BECOMING

A YOUNG MAN OF GOD

KEN RAWSON

AN 8-WEEK CURRICULUM FOR MIDDLE SCHOOL GUYS

FOR AGES 11-14

 ZONDERVAN®

ZONDERVAN.com/
AUTHORTRACKER
follow your favorite authors

 youth
specialties

**youth
specialties**

Becoming a Young Man of God
Copyright 2008 by Ken Rawson

Youth Specialties resources, 300 S. Pierce St., El Cajon, CA 92020 are published by Zondervan, 5300 Patterson Ave. SE, Grand Rapids, MI 49530.

ISBN 978-0-310-27878-8

Cover design by Toolbox Studios
Interior design by Mark Novelli, IMAGO MEDIA

Printed in the United States of America

08 09 10 11 12 13 • 20 19 18 17 16 15 14 13 12 11 10 9 8 7 6 5 4 3 2

For Noah Riley—may you become and live as a man of God. I love you, son.

ACKNOWLEDGMENTS

I attended my first Youth Specialties national resource seminar during my freshman year of college, in the spring of 1995 in Springfield, Missouri, where Doug Fields was the presenter. From that first day of training I was hooked on Youth Specialties (YS) and had a silly dream I might one day be a YS author.

Had it not been for my sweet wife, Jen, I'd still be dreaming that dream. Her incredible series for middle school girls (*Becoming a Young Woman of God* and *Living as a Young Woman of God*) paved the way for my dream to become reality. Her constant love, encouragement, grace, stubbornness, and belief in me have shaped my relationship with God and are making me a better man, husband, father, and friend. I love you, Jennifer Dawn.

Thank you to my dad, Larry Stilgebouer, who is a living demonstration of God's faithfulness and has given me a Christ-like model of what it means to be a father and a husband. Thanks also to my other dad, Ron Harris, for helping me draw near to what it means to be a godly husband and dad.

Thanks to all of the youth coaches from Central Christian Church, San Jose, California, who believed in me when I was just a chubby, loud-mouthed, mohawked, skateboarding middle schooler—Doug and Renee Daggett, Ted and Karen Goddard, Lon and Carla Hansen, Tony and Delaine Catudal, Pete and Jean Fong, Don and Debbie Ferguson, Scott and Erica Serface, Trey Hinkle, Kim and Nancy Robbie, Danny Quezada, Sean Mixon, and the rest of the congregation who never gave up on me.

Thank you to my three youth ministers, Steve Spray, Joel Brown, and Jim Coddington, who each shaped important parts of my story. Thanks to David Mullins, Pat Sehl, Jim Smith, and Trevor Hinz, who shared so much of their lives with me and will always be my band of brothers. Your lives and teachings are woven throughout these pages.

Thank you to Les Christie for your constant encouragement and my connection to home when you're out in the Midwest. Thanks to Phil Weece for believing one day I would write, and thanks to Kirk Longhofer for helping fine-tune my writing and communication. Thanks to Steve "Jake" Jacobs for being a constant reminder of God's grace and serving as my own little slice of Mike Yaconelli.

Thank you to First United Methodist Church in Wichita, Kansas, for allowing me to serve alongside a great staff as I minister to middle school students and their families.

Thanks to Sean Meade for showing me how to go for my dreams and to Kurt Johnston for helping me make middle school ministry simpler and for encouraging Jen to publish her book.

Thanks to everyone at Youth Specialties and Zondervan who had a part in putting this together. You guys are incredible!

Lastly, thank you to Ciera, Noah, and Charis, who went without lots of wrestling, swimming, playing, and karaoke singing while I finished this project. You've taught me so much about what it means to be a man and a dad, and I love you very, very much.

CONTENTS

INTRODUCTION: THE PUZZLE OF MANHOOD

Before the first tuft of hair escapes from the sweaty armpit of an 11-year-old boy, he's already confused about what it means for him to be a man. Throughout their brief early-adolescent years (11-14), boys are given different puzzle pieces, each one inscribed with information about the meaning of being a man.

Some pieces are from their fathers. Other pieces are from other adults, friends, and especially the media. In the end, our middle school boys sit at a metaphorical card table with a bad leg, attempting to put all these pieces together without the real picture on the box top to guide them.

Often their picture of real manhood looks this way:

Real men are tough athletes and fast runners, have six-pack abs, can bench-press at the very least their own weight, hit home runs, score touchdowns, have a bunch of girlfriends, climb rocks without harnesses, ride choppers, have cool cars, marry a trophy wife, end up with successful jobs making lots of money, and retire independently wealthy.

Then they're given a tattered baggie of worn-out puzzle pieces related to what Christian men are—that they're wishy-washy, go to church every day and evening, carry their Bibles with them everywhere, never even look at females, wear ties and pocket protectors, drive minivans, and stay at home the rest of the time.

This can't be what God had in mind.

Exactly! It's not.

And that's where *Becoming a Young Man of God* comes into play. It consists of eight sessions focusing on the truth about what a young man of God thinks (head), feels (heart), and does (hands). In your time together you'll attempt to strip away your guys' false ideas of male identity and rebuild a solid biblical foundation to help them become young men of God.

Before you jump in, briefly go over each element of the sessions. Also read the three tips to make the most of this resource.

SESSION ELEMENTS

At the beginning of each session **The Big Idea, Main Text**, and **What's the Point?** give the main Bible passage for the week and a brief overview of the focus of what you're teaching that week.

YOU'LL NEED

This list shows *everything* you might need to teach the session—depending on which of the many options you choose for various session sections. In other words, you may not need everything listed; skim through the chapter to find the options you like and make sure you have the supplies for those. In addition to what's listed, you'll nearly always need Bibles, pens, and copies of the reproducible pages at the end of the chapter.

RECAP SOUL WORK

See **Soul Work** explanation later in the **Introduction**.

OPENING ACTIVITY

Here you're given some options for introducing the week's session to your guys. These activities are fun ways to get your students focused on where you're headed.

The Big Picture

This is the main point you're trying to get across. This is easily the most focused time of your teaching. Each session has an **Outline** sheet for the guys to follow for the **Big Picture**. If you're short on time, you might use your version of the **Outline**—the **Outline (Leader Guide)**—as your main lesson and pick and choose from the other options to fine-tune your time together. You'll find the **Outline (Leader Guide)** at the end of each chapter with the reproducible handouts. It includes everything on the guys' sheet with some suggestions in parentheses to help you explain the ideas.

Breakdown

This is where you flesh out the idea presented in the **Big Picture** and give your guys time to wrestle with it.

Closing Activity

This section gives your guys real-world applications for what you just taught them—something practical they can do in response to what they learned—or take-home reminders.

Soul Work

At the end of each session, you'll give your guys a short take-home assignment called **Soul Work** that'll whet their appetites for the next week's session. You can also begin each week with a review of the previous week's **Soul Work**, using the section called **Recap Soul Work.**

THREE TIPS TO HELP YOU MAKE THE MOST OF BECOMING A YOUNG MAN OF GOD

1. Make It Yours

There are a lot of options for each of the sessions—more than you'll probably have time for. Go through each chapter and use what will best connect with your students. Add your own stories and show appropriate transparency. Don't force the lessons. Tweak them and make them fit your group of guys, your context. If all you have is 10 minutes, use the **Outline** and the **Big Picture** section. If you want to show video clips every week, do that.

2. Have Fun

My guys connect better and pay more attention when I marry the lesson with having fun. Use some of the games to introduce your session. Tell funny or embarrassing stories from when you were their age. Eleven- to 14-year-old guys need appropriate outlets to diffuse their energy and help them process. Use the different options in the chapters to help direct some of that energy and help the guys stay connected.

3. Take a Week Off

Every four weeks I schedule a "week off" from teaching my guys. We'll do three weeks of Bible study or session study in small groups, and then take one week off. For this week off I still meet with my guys, but we go out and do something together—play video games, minigolf, hang out at the park, race go-carts, or go out to eat.

What's Next?

When your guys are done with *Becoming a Young Man of God,* challenge them to take the next step by offering *Living as a Young Man of God,* where we'll take a look at other important issues guys struggle with and learn how Jesus dealt with them. *Living as a Young Man of God* is another eight-week series dealing with feelings, girls, friends, dads, and other topics. Each session focuses on Jesus as our ultimate model of what it means to live as a young man of God.

THANK YOU

Before you jump into this resource, I want to thank you for making a difference in the lives of your guys. Your notes, e-mails, phone calls, and the time you spend before and after teaching are shaping their souls and character.

I pray that as you finish this resource, your guys will develop an unparalleled sense of trust, vulnerability, and love for each other in your group. I also pray they'll become godly young men—which in turn will not only radically transform their home life, but will also help them someday become better husbands and fathers who'll share the love of Christ with their children and grandchildren.

Lastly, I pray you'll be able to use this resource as a reliable "box top" in helping your guys put together all the pieces in the "puzzle of manhood." (At the very least you can use the book to prop up that bad table leg!)

CHAPTER ONE

BREAKING THE CODE: TAKING OFF THE MASK

THE BIG IDEA

The mask boys wear more than any other can be summed up in two words: "Everything's fine." If you ask a boy how he's doing, even in the worst of his pain, his answer will most likely be, "Everything's fine." It's time to take off the mask and get to the core of each of your guys.

Main Text

> If others think they have reasons to put confidence in the flesh, I have more: circumcised on the eighth day, of the people of Israel, of the tribe of Benjamin, a Hebrew of Hebrews; in regard to the law, a Pharisee; as for zeal, persecuting the church; as for righteousness based on the law, faultless. But whatever were gains to me I now consider loss for the sake of Christ. What is more, I consider everything a loss because of the surpassing worth of knowing Christ Jesus my Lord, for whose sake I have lost all things. I consider them garbage, that I may gain Christ. (Philippians 3:4-8)

What's the Point?

Guys are conditioned very early into a certain code of conduct: "Be tough." "Don't cry." "Don't be a wimp." "Don't play with dolls." You know the drill. We're conditioned to hide our feelings and our true selves. In this session we'll expose this code and help students recognize it as a mask guys hide behind. We'll challenge them to take off that mask and risk the opportunity to find life beyond the code. We'll show them they don't have to fit the mold to be godly young men.

OPENING ACTIVITY

Option One: Quiz—How Manly Are You?

This quiz is utterly ridiculous. It's meant to be! It's a great way to point out our culture's crazy ideas of "manly" behavior. Use the quiz as a launching point for a great discussion on what it really means to be a man.

Welcome your boys and say something like, **Hey, I'm glad you're here. We're getting ready to jump into a series about what it means to be a man. But before we can talk about what it means to be a man, we need to take a quiz to see how manly you really are.**

Pass out the quiz.

Transition from the quiz to the **Big Picture** by asking some of the following questions:

▷ **Which question on the quiz did you think was the funniest?**

▷ **Would a real man do any or all of the things on the quiz?**

▷ **Who decides what makes someone a real man or not?**

▷ **What do you think a real man *is* like?**

Move to the **Big Picture** by saying, **Obviously, this quiz isn't meant seriously. However, a lot of people, a lot of men, would say some of these ridiculous ideas are correct. Some men might even agree that these answers are ridiculous, but when push comes to shove, they really believe these qualities make someone manly. Today we'll take a look at a guy who *was* a real man.**

Option Two: The Manly List

Say to your guys, **Today we're starting to talk about what it means to be a man. There are many ideas out there, and the Bible has a ton to say about what it means to be a man. But first let's brainstorm and talk about what we think it means to be a manly man.**

Using your chalkboard, whiteboard, or butcher paper, have students make a list of what they think it means to be a man today. You might get guys who are being "churchy" with answers such as "reads his Bible" or "goes to church." If you do, challenge them to think of different areas. C'mon—they're guys! They're already compartmentalizing! But help them work with the idea.

There's nothing wrong with "nice" answers, either, though. Put those on the list and ask the guys for more. Don't let them off the hook. Push them to think of what our culture says manhood is all about.

Here are some examples, and you can think of more yourself. If your guys are really quiet, you can direct the discussion with your examples.

A real manly, burly dude—

▷ is tough.

▷ is funny.

▷ reads his Bible.

▷ has lots of money.

▷ is godly.

▷ drives a great car.

▷ has girls hanging all over him.

▷ plays with his kids.

▷ drinks beer.

▷ is good at sports.

▷ is totally smart.

▷ owns his own business.

▷ is ripped with muscles.

Then ask some of the following questions:

▷ **Of all the items on the list, which ones do you think are really true?**

▷ **Of all the items on the list, which ones do you think are real jokes?**

▷ **Where do we get our ideas about what makes a man?**

▷ **Where should we get our understanding of what a manly man is?**

Transition your guys to the **Big Picture** by saying something like, **There are all kinds of ideas about what it takes to be a really manly guy, whether it's making lots of money or riding a chopper and having a ton of tattoos. We all need to know what it means to be real men. Today we'll take a look at a guy who** *was* **a real man.**

Option Three: A Story from Your Life

Welcome your guys and let them know that today and throughout your times together, you'll be focused around the idea of becoming real men.

Share what growing up was like for you. Share how you grew up and what you thought it meant to be a man. Did something about your dad or the men in your family kind of drive you to become the man you are now? What were some of the myths you fell for about what it means to be a man, and what did they cost you? Who in your life demonstrated godly manhood to you? How did you come to realize what a man is supposed to be?

Share stories from your life to illustrate the idea that what you thought it meant to be a man and what you came to understand as godly manhood were either right on or polar opposites or a mix of both.

Feel free to let students ask you questions. They may not, but you might be able to initiate some discussion by saying something like, **Have any of you guys ever felt some of those things or thought some of those things?** Then ask them to share times when they could relate to your story.

Remember, the objective of the **Opening Activity** is to get your guys to question what they've always thought being a man means and to spark their interest in what you and God have to say about manhood.

Tip: If you feel your story would make a better conclusion, then save it for later. Maybe you can split it into two parts. Share about what you used to think being a man meant for the opener. Then share at the end about what you know now about being a man.

After you're done, transition to the **Big Picture** by saying something like, **We all have our own ideas about what it means to be real men. Today we're going to look at the Bible and one guy who** *was* **a real man**.

THE BIG PICTURE

Abstract Alert: This idea of wearing a mask to pretend you're someone else is pretty easy to understand at Halloween. But talking about the invisible masks we all wear every day may take some of your students to the edge of their thinking ability. However, this is a key and fundamental concept we'll come back to often, so take the time to help them understand this now.

The mask boys wear more than any other can be summed up in two words: "Everything's fine." If you ask a boy how he's doing, even in the worst of his pain, his answer will most likely be, "Everything's fine."

Options One and Two are good openers for discussing the issue, but where we really dig into this idea is **Option Three**. If your guys are up to it, have fun using option one or two, then use option three to dig into this issue as much as possible.

If you have younger teenagers, just be familiar with the third option and squeeze as much as you can out of one of the two first options and before you move to the **Breakdown**.

Option One: Taking Off the Mask

Take out your mask and have your guys each try on the mask (or masks if you brought more than one). Have some fun with the guys; take pictures of them being goofy if you brought a camera.

Then open the discussion with these questions:

▷ **Why are masks so fun to wear? What are some of the fun things you can do with masks?** *(Possible answers: No one can see who you are. No one knows who you are. You can pretend to be someone you aren't. You can do things you wouldn't normally do.)*

▷ **Who are some famous superheroes who wear masks?** *(the Lone Ranger, Batman, Spider-Man, etc.)*

▷ **Why do they wear masks?** *(To protect their secret identities. If certain people knew who the heroes were, they might harm the heroes' loved ones. If people knew who the heroes really were, people might not like the heroes. People might only like them because they're superheroes and not like their real selves. To protect themselves.)*

Move to the **Breakdown** by saying, **When it comes to being men, many of us hide behind masks because we're afraid of what would happen if people knew who we really are. Some people hide behind masks of being tough, rich, funny, athletic, etc. Next I'm going to introduce you to a guy who refused to hide behind any mask.**

Option Two: *Nacho Libre*

The story: Jack Black plays a monk named Nacho who loves professional wrestling and wants to win a tournament so he can buy better food for the children in the orphanage where he grew up and now works. Unfortunately, the monks believe wrestling is a sin because of all the things it's associated with: women, greed, etc.

Note: For this clip use the English subtitles to help the guys pick up on what Nacho says. Show this clip from chapter four (start the clip at 25:28 and end the clip at 29:07, "Don't worry. I won't tell anybody.")

Ask these questions:

▷ **You can hardly understand it, but Nacho says, "I couldn't let anyone see me without my mask." Why does Nacho need a mask?** *(He has to keep his identity a secret from the other monks.)*

▷ **How does Nacho change when he wears the mask?** *(He feels stronger and braver than he does without the mask.)* **Nacho says, "Do you remember when everyone was cheering my name and I ripped my blouse?... I felt a power deep inside me. Something I had never felt before."**

▷ **What would happen if his mask were to come off?** *(People would know he's just the weird guy at the monastery, the orphan nobody wanted. They wouldn't think he was great or anything.)*

Move to the **Breakdown** by saying, **When it comes to being men, many of us hide behind masks because we're afraid of what would happen if people knew who we really are. We think our masks will give us power of some sort. Some people hide behind masks of being tough, rich, funny, athletic, etc. Next I'm going to introduce you to a guy who refused to hide behind any mask.**

DEVO ON NACHO

While Nacho felt powerful with the mask on, it didn't help him at all. Nacho got beaten up. Steven even says, "You got knocked unconscious." So even though he felt powerful with the mask, it was just a prop and really didn't change him at all.

If you need or want
another good choice for
illustrating the power
behind a mask, use Jim
Carrey's *The Mask*. It's a
fun story about a hum-
ble, quiet guy who finds
an ancient mask that
gives him super powers
when he wears it. (Start
the clip at 00:16:48,
"So, Dr. Newman, you're
saying that everybody
wears masks?" Stop at
00:19:50, "Look, Ma, I'm
road kill! Ha, ha, ha.")

Follow-up questions:

1. How does Stanley
change when he wears
the mask?

2. What does Dr. New-
man mean by "We all
wear masks"?

3. What kinds of masks
do guys wear?

4. How do the masks
we wear make us able
to do things we normally
wouldn't do

Option Three: The Code

Help your guys begin thinking about masks by asking these questions:

▷ **You're riding your bike and fall and hurt yourself. Someone asks if you're all right. What do you say?**

▷ **You've recently broken up with your girlfriend and are pretty bummed. Your parents notice it right away and ask, "Are you okay?" What do you say?**

▷ **You get into a fight at school. A bully pops you in the mouth, and you fall to the ground. The fight breaks up, and your friend or a teacher helps you up. The first words out of your mouth are...?**

Their answers can probably be summed up in two words: "Everything's fine." Share briefly about the "boy code."

Welcome to the "boy code"[1]: Everything's fine. That's what guys want everyone to believe. We're in control. We're okay. Everything's fine. Even when it's not. If you're a guy, this is the code you live by.

Now ask, **How's the code—the idea that we're always in control, everything's fine—like a mask?** After some answers say, **Here are three ways:**

1. **We hide behind the code. If everything's not fine, then we'd be saying we need help. We hide our deepest thoughts and feelings.**

2. **The code, the mask, protects us from getting hurt. It keeps people thinking we're tough.**

3. **The mask of the code makes sure we fit in. It makes us normal. If we don't wear the mask, people will think we're weird. If we fit in, we'll be loved.**

Then ask, **Why do guys mask their feelings?**

[1] William Pollack coined this term and idea in his book *Real Boys. Rescuing Our Sons from the Myths of Boyhood.* New York: Owl Books, 1998.

Hint: Don't be surprised if you end up with the same answer—"I don't know"—even after you give them the answers about the code. This is a hard teaching. Many of us have been conditioned to feel bad, actually to feel shame, for having feelings. We aren't supposed to cry. We're supposed to be tough!

After you get some answers, transition to the **Breakdown** by saying something like, **The mask of the code is a lie. Everything isn't always fine. Everything isn't always okay. Everything isn't always all right. When you decide to "break the code" and take off the mask, then you're ready to experience real life. And real life is found in a relationship with God.**

BREAKDOWN

Now that your guys have an idea about what the code is and how guys hide behind masks, share with them about the apostle Paul and how he could've hidden his life behind so many masks, yet he refused.

Say something like, **Paul was a man among men for a lot of reasons. When we first encounter him in the Bible, his name is actually Saul, and he takes part in the murder of one of the church's first leaders, Stephen. He's so intense about his belief in God that when Christians come on the scene saying there's a new God called Jesus, Saul takes it upon himself to kill as many Christians as possible.**

Continue, **But something happens to Saul. He meets Jesus. Saul gets a new name, Paul, and becomes a Christian and one of the most important Christian leaders in history. As a matter of fact, he wrote most of the New Testament.**

Share with your guys about Paul and then go through the **Outline** together.

CLOSING ACTIVITY
Option One: War Story

If you haven't shared a story from your life about this manhood confusion, you may choose to close out your time together with one. Share about how you've come to understand this whole issue of hiding behind masks and making Christ the centerpiece of your life.

After your story go over the **Soul Work** assignment page and close in prayer.

Option Two: Bandannas

Give each of your guys a bandanna to make a mask from, as they did in the old Westerns when the bad guys would hold up stagecoaches. Have each guy put on and then take off his mask.

Share with the guys that these bandannas are theirs to keep as reminders to be brave enough to take off their masks. Encourage each guy to put the mask somewhere he'll see it every day, such as on his bedpost, dresser, or mirror.

Go over the **Soul Work** assignment page and close in prayer.

BREAKING THE CODE: TAKING OFF THE MASK

1. Breaking the Code

    A. The boy code = <u>everything's</u> <u>fine</u>.

    B. But everything isn't fine.

    C. Real life = <u>knowing</u> Christ.

FIRST THING

One of the coolest guys in the Bible is Paul. He and another guy named Peter are the main leaders after Jesus goes back to heaven. Think of them as the two guys in charge.

Christianity is brand new, and all kinds of people are trying to lead the church and tell everyone what they need to believe.

Can you imagine someone who'd never played basketball coaching a basketball team? Or someone who'd never seen a TV trying to build one? That's kind of what's going on. People are trying to lead this new religion, even though they know little about it.

Peter and Paul know all about Jesus personally and about what God's trying to do. These other people don't have a clue. But the people who are trying to lead push their weight around by saying and showing how religious they are. They wear "masks" to make themselves look more spiritual than they really are.

SECOND THING

Read Philippians 3:4-8 and fill in number 2A to G together.

> If others think they have reasons to put confidence in the flesh, I have more: circumcised on the eighth day, of the people of Israel, of the tribe of Benjamin, a Hebrew of Hebrews; in regard to the law, a Pharisee; as for zeal, persecuting the church; as for righteousness based on the law, faultless. But whatever were gains to me I now consider loss for the sake of Christ. What is more, I consider everything a loss because of the surpassing worth of knowing Christ Jesus my Lord, for whose sake I have lost all things. I consider them garbage, that I may gain Christ. (Philippians 3:4-8)

2. Paul states seven hard-core reasons why he knows what he's talking about:

   A. <u>Circumcised</u> on the eighth day (Ouch!) (His parents kept the law of Moses.)

   B. Of the people of <u>Israel</u> (God's chosen people)

   C. Tribe of <u>Benjamin</u> (Deuteronomy 33:12: "The beloved of the LORD.")

   D. Hebrew of Hebrews (The first three things make him a Hebrew of Hebrews.)

   E. <u>Pharisee</u> (Religious leader.)

   F. Zealous (Willing to kill Christians for the cause.)

   G. <u>Faultless</u> (No one has any dirt on this guy.)

Paul is a religious powerhouse. You don't want to mess with him. But do any of those things matter to him? NO!

3. What does matter to Paul? <u>Knowing</u> Christ.

4. Compared to knowing Christ, everything else is (<u>loss, worthless, garbage, etc.</u>).

Look at how another Bible version—*The Message*—describes it:

> The very credentials these people are waving around as something special, I'm tearing up and throwing out with the trash—along with everything else I used to take credit for. And why? Because of Christ. Yes, all the things I once thought were so important are gone from my life. Compared to the high privilege of knowing Christ Jesus as my Master, firsthand, everything I once thought I had going for me is insignificant—dog dung. I've dumped it all in the trash so that I could embrace Christ and be embraced by him. I didn't want some petty, inferior brand of righteousness that comes from keeping a list of rules when I could get the robust kind that comes from trusting Christ—God's righteousness. (Philippians 3:7-9)

5. Why would Paul say the only thing that matters is knowing Christ?

Being a man isn't about being tough, cool, macho, funny, good-looking, or smart.

You don't have to date the cheerleader, sink the shot at the buzzer, or drive a cool car.

Being a man isn't about being a loner, a rebel, or the homecoming king.

Being a man isn't about pretending "Everything's fine. I'm okay. I'm invincible."

Being a man is about two things:

1. Taking off the mask.

2. Knowing Christ.

MANLY QUIZ

HOW MANLY ARE YOU?

Choose the answer that demonstrates the most manliness.

Example: You're driving in a town you aren't very familiar with. In fact, you're lost and have been for two hours. What do you do?

A. Pray God will direct your path.

B. Stop at the nearest store and ask for directions.

C. Stop, pull out the map you packed, and get back on the right path.

D. Map? Who needs a map? Keep driving till you find the place. You don't need any help!

1. You've found a brown recluse spider in your kitchen. As a real man, you—

   A. swat that bugger and listen for the crunch.

   B. safely capture the spider and release it outside.

   C. pull off each leg slowly and torture the spider till it dies a slow, cruel death.

   D. put the spider in your underwear and do jumping jacks while taunting it to do its worst. Let it bite you and inject poison into your body. Then eat it and laugh out loud at your triumph.

2. Your mom lets you pick a movie to rent. As a real man, you rent—

   A. a romantic comedy.

   B. a Western.

   C. a horror flick.

   D. anything with lots of violence.

3. Your dad is working on the car. To show him how manly you are, you:

   A. bring him a glass of water.

   B. go out and give him a hand.

   C. tell him all the things he's doing wrong and show him how it's really done.

   D. tell your dad to go get you a glass of water, and you'll finish up the mess he's created.

4. You're having a catch with your dad. How do you play?

   A. You throw each ball perfectly so he doesn't even have to move his mitt.

   B. You demonstrate your mad fielding skills and accurate gun.

   C. You throw every pitch with intense velocity.

   D. You throw curves, sliders, knucklers, and fastballs without letting your dad give you any signs—he has to guess what's coming down the pike.

5. There's a school dance coming up, and you need a date. Who do you ask?

   A. What dance? You don't dance. You ain't getting on the dance floor.

   B. You ask your cousin Melva to go with you.

   C. You ask a girl from church to go with you—you know, just as (ugh) "friends."

   D. You go up to the best-looking girl at school and tell her when you're picking her up for the dance.

6. You're at your friend's house, and his parents are gone. He's gotten hold of their liquor stash and asks if you want a drink. Of course, as a real man, you—

   A. remind him you're underage.

   B. say you'd love to but you've got to get home.

   C. have a sip at least—what harm can that do?

   D. get drunk.

7. You're out riding motorcycles and bail hard. Your knee is cut pretty badly and is bleeding a ton. What's a man's man supposed to do?

   A. Cry. Like a little girl. Wah! Boo-hoo!

   B. Assess the situation and ask someone to call for help.

   C. Hold your knee, grit your teeth, get up, and limp off the course.

   D. First, lick your wound. Second, pack it with lots of fresh dirt. Third, ask, "What are you looking at?" Fourth, get back on your bike and try it again.

8. Guys have to collect stuff. Which of these collections doesn't belong?

 A. guns

 B. knives

 C. LEGOs

 D. Barbies

9. Everyone's talking about sex—who's having it, how many times, with whom, and what ways. The talk finally comes to you. You confess:

 A. "This is lame. You guys are all full of garbage. Did you see the game last night?"

 B. "Well, uh, guys, actually, uh, I'm a, well, you see, uh, I've never really, uh, you know… what I'm trying to say, is that…I haven't, uh…I'm a…a…a…[very quietly] virgin."

 C. "I've done it a couple of times."

 D. "When am I *not* having sex is the question!"

10. The school bully has finally knocked on the wrong door—yours. He wants you, and he's not waiting 'til after school. It's happening now, right in front of everyone at lunch. The teachers aren't paying attention. As he winds up to punch you, you—

 A. start crying and run away.

 B. tell him you don't believe in violence and won't fight.

 C. dodge his punches and protect yourself from getting hurt as much as possible.

 D. scissor-kick him in the face like they do in those *Matrix* movies. Now that he's stunned, you jump off a table, landing on top of him where you decide to crush him like mashed potatoes. Students give you a standing ovation, and teachers come up to shake your hand for taking care of their problem—but you're too busy giving your victim the double fishhook to notice.

BREAKING THE CODE: TAKING OFF THE MASK

1. Breaking the Code

   A. The boy code = e_____ f_____.

   B. But everything isn't fine.

   C. Real life = k_____ Christ.

FIRST THING

One of the coolest guys in the Bible is a guy named Paul. He and another guy named Peter are the two main leaders after Jesus goes back to heaven. Think of them as the two guys in charge.

Christianity is brand new, and all kinds of people are trying to lead the church and tell everyone what they need to believe.

Can you imagine someone who'd never played basketball coaching a basketball team? Or someone who'd never seen a TV trying to build one? That's kind of what's going on. People are trying to lead this new religion, even though they know little about it.

Peter and Paul know all about Jesus personally and about what God's trying to do. These other people don't have a clue. But the people who are trying to lead push their weight around by saying and showing how religious they are. They wear "masks" to make themselves look more spiritual than they really are.

SECOND THING

Read Philippians 3:4-8 and fill in number 2A to G together.

> If others think they have reasons to put confidence in the flesh, I have more: circumcised on the eighth day, of the people of Israel, of the tribe of Benjamin, a Hebrew of Hebrews; in regard to the law, a Pharisee; as for zeal, persecuting the church; as for righteousness based on the law, faultless. But whatever were gains to me I now consider loss for the sake of Christ. What is more, I consider everything a loss because of the surpassing worth of knowing Christ Jesus my Lord, for whose sake I have lost all things. I consider them garbage, that I may gain Christ. (Philippians 3:4-8)

2. Paul states seven hard-core reasons why he knows what he's talking about:

    A. C_____ on the eighth day (Ouch!)

    B. Of the people of I_____

    C. Tribe of B_____

    D. Hebrew of Hebrews

    E. P_____

    F. Zealous

    G. F_____

Paul is a religious powerhouse. You don't want to mess with him. But do any of those things matter to him? NO!

3. What does matter to Paul? K_____ Christ.

4. Compared to knowing Christ, everything else is _____.

Look at how another Bible version—*The Message*—describes it:

> The very credentials these people are waving around as something special, I'm tearing up and throwing out with the trash—along with everything else I used to take credit for. And why? Because of Christ. Yes, all the things I once thought were so important are gone from my life. Compared to the high privilege of knowing Christ Jesus as my Master,

firsthand, everything I once thought I had going for me is insignificant—dog dung. I've dumped it all in the trash so that I could embrace Christ and be embraced by him. I didn't want some petty, inferior brand of righteousness that comes from keeping a list of rules when I could get the robust kind that comes from trusting Christ—God's righteousness. (Philippians 3:7-9)

5. Why would Paul say the only thing that matters is knowing Christ?

Being a man isn't about being tough, cool, macho, funny, good-looking, or smart.

You don't have to date the cheerleader, sink the shot at the buzzer, or drive a cool car.

Being a man isn't about being a loner, a rebel, or the homecoming king.

Being a man isn't about pretending "Everything's fine. I'm okay. I'm invincible."

Being a man is about two things:

1. Taking off the mask.

2. Knowing Christ.

MEN IN THE MEDIA

Your **Soul Work** for this week is to watch TV. Ah, yeah, I know what you're saying: "This is my kind of homework!" Only one small catch—I need you to think critically while you watch TV and fill out the following chart.

So pick some shows with guy characters who seem really cool or manly. Then write down why you think each guy is a cool dude or what makes him really "manly." Check out the example, then fill in yours underneath.

Name of TV show	Who is the man?	What makes him "manly"?
24	Jack Bauer	The dude always saves the day. He's totally smart and cool under pressure. And he looks cool.

CHAPTER TWO

WILL THE REAL SLIM SHADY PLEASE STAND UP? MEDIA VERSUS REALITY

THE BIG IDEA

Where do you get your self-worth?

Main text

> See to it that no one takes you captive through hollow and deceptive philosophy, which depends on human tradition and the elemental spiritual forces of this world rather than on Christ. (Colossians 2:8)

What's the Point?

Eminem raps about people trying to be like him and impersonating him—which is ironic since he exists by impersonating, of all people, himself. He's a creation of what the media has said he needs to be. He's lost touch with who he really is and has become a caricature of what people expect.

This isn't unlike what our own guys go through. Our hope is they'll separate themselves from what the media says they need to be, and then their real selves will be able to stand up.

This week we'll take a look at how the media in our culture views what a man is and how he's supposed to behave. We'll point out the emptiness the media portrays and contrast that with the incredible value God places on each one of us.

RECAP SOUL WORK

Last week's **Soul Work** was all about media and TV. The assignment was to watch TV and evaluate the men in the shows and what makes them manly.

Go through the students' assessments and see how they did. If they didn't end up doing the **Soul Work**, try to talk about which TV shows they're familiar with. This will help you lead in to today's session.

Don't forget to reward your guys if they did their assignments. Give them credit and really pump them up. Make it a big deal that they followed through.

OPENING ACTIVITY
Option One: Manly Movie

Welcome your guys with some high fives and tell them you want to show them a sweet clip from one of your favorite movies. Show your students five to 10 minutes of whichever very manly movie you've picked and ask them some of these questions:

▷ **In this short clip, how would you describe the main character?** *(Possible answers: courageous, strong, powerful, handsome, manly, fighter, brave, the hero, etc.)*

▷ **Can you name some other guy-type movies with hero kinds of guys?**

▷ **What makes these guys so cool?** *(They're the heroes. Everyone loves them. They get the girls. They're the superstars.)*

▷ **Are these guys real?** *(No. No one is really like these guys.)*

Transition your guys to the next part by saying something like, **Today we're going to enter the battle of media versus reality. We'll look at how the media portrays guys—in movies, music, TV, magazines, etc. Let's jump in.**

Pray and go to the **Big Picture.**

Option Two: Extra Time

Let me begin by saying if you can pull this off, you're the man! This will be so sweet. Grab five to 10 of your favorite guy movies and tape them or copy some of your favorite scenes so you have five to 10 minutes of absolute testosterone-fueled video clips. (If you want an easier way to do this, you can find clips on the Internet, such as YouTube.)

Welcome your guys and tell them to name some of their favorite guy movies and why they like those movies.

Once they're done sharing, begin to tell them some of yours...then stop and say, **Instead of telling you about my favorites, I want to show you a little something I think will help me tell you more about them.**

Throw in the tape or DVD or show the clip from the Internet and enjoy your masterpiece. After your students give you a standing ovation for the time you devoted to making this compilation, lead them through the questions and transition from **Option One.**

Option Three: War Story

When you share from your life, you build credibility and trust with your students. Think back to when you were a boy or teenager and some of the men who were heroes in your life.

For me it was two guys: Bobcat Goldthwaite and Brutus the Barber Beefcake. Bobcat was just the craziest guy. He was so funny. And Brutus, well, he was a World Wrestling Federation star with awesome hair and a killer finishing move—the sleeper hold.

Nevertheless, these guys symbolized true manhood to me: A man made people laugh. Gave people joy. That's the kind of person I wanted to be. I also thought men had to be tough. Have big muscles. Be able to protect others and fight the bad guys. Never be afraid.

You may be thinking I'm the biggest dork, and I probably am, but those guys helped define what a man was for me. Maybe for you it was a different sports hero—Hulk Hogan, Arnold Schwarzenegger, or your dad.

Share with your guys who some of those men were or are and why those guys are so important to you. How did they shape your idea of manliness and where a guy gets his self-worth?

Then ask your guys some of these questions:

▷ I've shared with you guys some of my heroes as a boy. Who are some of yours?

▷ What makes these guys so cool?

▷ Based on these heroes, what do you think a real man should be like?

▷ Where should a man get his value from?

Take them to the next step by saying, **We're going to take a closer look at media—at how guys are portrayed in movies, TV, and music—and what that says about what a man should be today.**

Open your time up with prayer and head to the **Big Picture.**

THE BIG PICTURE
Option One: Make a Collage

Note: This is a great exercise for guys to do, so take the time necessary to let them really dig into this stuff.

Give your guys a bunch of pages from guy magazines (*Warning:* Make sure the content is appropriate, as well as specific to the five upcoming questions) and scissors and give them these instructions: **I want you to pretend you're aliens, and you just landed here in a spaceship to study human guys. However, you just scared them, and they've all deserted the place. You still have five questions you need answered, but all you have to answer them with are these magazine pages. Cut out or tear out the pictures, words, and articles you feel answer these five questions.** You can ask the questions aloud or write them on a posterboard or whiteboard, etc.

1. What kinds of guys are respected, well thought of?

2. What is the normal build for a guy? How's he supposed to look?

3. What is a male's role? What's his job?

4. What happens when a man doesn't fit this role or appearance?

5. What are guys' interests? What do guys do?

REWARDS

Build rewards into your small group. I reward my guys for answering questions and bringing their Bibles, notebooks, friends, etc. It doesn't have to be much. Anything you can give to motivate positive behavior is a winner. Here are a few ideas:

• *Stickers*: You can make homemade stickers by taking some fun photos, printing them on mailing labels, and then cutting them out. It seems hokey, but guys dig them in a sticker-on-your-football-helmet kind of way.

• *Coupons*: Fast-food places are always willing to give away coupons for free ice cream, soda, etc. Call up your favorite place and get some rewards.

• *Candy*: the staple. You can't go wrong with candy. (Of course, their parents might not be as thankful.)

Once your guys have gone through the magazine pages and are satisfied with their answers, go through the five questions together. While they answer, paste their pictures, words, and article headings onto the posterboard. When you're done, you'll have made a great collage you'll be able to refer to throughout this series.

Next hit them with these questions:

▷ **What does this tell you about your value as a man?**

▷ **How do you feel about that?**

▷ **What other false values does our culture or the media hold about guys?**

Transition to the meat of the study by saying, **None of these things makes up what a man's supposed to be. The media is a joke. It isn't real. Let's take a look at what God says about what a guy is supposed to be.**

Option Two: Do Your Own Collage

If you feel like there's NO WAY your guys are going to sit down and do **Option One**, you might consider just making a collage yourself.

So go through the same exercise on your own and make your own collage. Bring it with you and tell your guys what you did. Then walk them through the whole alien situation and have them answer the questions based on the collage you made.

You'll still be able to lead them through the pointlessness of our culture's definition of manliness without the distraction of tearing up magazine pages and cutting out pictures.

So go through the questions from **Option One** and the transition to the **Breakdown**.

Option Three: TV Collage

Am I a sucker for TV or what? Maybe. But I know my middle school boys are, too. If you have a little extra time, you can create a really cool experience for them.

Tape about an hour of TV. Spike TV would be even better than regular TV channels to illustrate our point. But if you don't have cable, just tape an hour of late-night TV or sports programming. If you aren't tech savvy, get someone to help you with the next part.

Go through and edit out all the programs. Pick out four to six different commercials and have them play all in a row. You've just created a video collage.

Next go through the same exercises as in **Option One**—walk them through the whole alien situation and have them answer the questions based on the commercials they just watched. After your discussion, go to the **Breakdown**.

BREAKDOWN

Find some "before and after" photos of famous people on the Internet (which show how makeup and airbrushing can make anyone look better, because reality is usually pretty scary) and show them to your guys. There's one of Arnold Schwarzenegger at the beach that's particularly frightening—find it and use it.

Pass out today's **Outline** and say, **The hardest part about media is that it's just not real. No one can measure up to what it shows. If you base your worth, your self-worth, on what the media tells us a man is, you'll never become a man.**

Go through the photos and talk about the particulars of each—how, for instance, some people get tons of makeup, others hide parts of their bodies, etc. Then say, **Lastly, we have good ol' Arnie (Arnold Schwarzenegger). The point is, here was this macho man of a guy. Mr. Universe. But even Mr. Universe gets old and can't maintain the manly man image forever.**

If you have access to a computer and can utilize PowerPoint, you'll really be able to emphasize the dramatic changes by toggling back and forth between before-and-after pictures using the arrows. If you're stuck using only printouts, it's all good. You'll just have to work a little harder to point out the differences between the photos.

After everyone has checked out the photos, point them to today's **Outline**. Once you've gone through the **Outline**—and your students have decided to throw their televisions into the trash, along with their CDs, movies, and all things that may destroy their new God-centered self-image (okay...maybe not, but we're getting closer)—you can move right to the **Closing Activity** to make your talk stick in their brains.

NO TIME FOR EDITING?

No problem! Find a part in the tape where you get three or four commercials in a row. They might not all fit what you're trying to communicate, but surely one or two will.

Now instead of using magazines, watch the commercial montage you created with your guys and then go through the whole alien exercise and questions in **Option One**.

CLOSING ACTIVITY

Option One: Eminem

Say, **One of Eminem's songs, "The Real Slim Shady," goes like this:**

> **I'm Slim Shady, yes, I'm the real Shady**
>
> **All you other Slim Shadys are just imitating**
>
> **So won't the real Slim Shady please stand up,**
>
> **please stand up, please stand up?**

I don't encourage playing the song or video since it's pretty graphic.

After you read the lyrics, say something like, **What's ironic is that even though Eminem is introducing himself to all the listeners in this song, he doesn't know who he really is. He's the creation of what the media has tagged a "gangsta rapper."**

Continue, **Eminem was at one point the top rapper in the industry. Now he's just another rapper in the sea of entertainers. And one day he won't be a rapper anymore. He'll just be Marshall Mathers** (Eminem's real name).

Then say, **My prayer is that Marshall will someday know what you guys now know—you're valuable because God created you and Jesus Christ died for you.**

Go over the **Soul Work** assignment for this week and close in prayer, asking God to remind each of you of your value and identity this week.

Option Two: *You Are Special* Book

Check out the book by Max Lucado titled *You Are Special*. If you have the extra time, read the book.

This is a GREAT illustration of exactly what we're talking about. Punchinello is a toy who wants people to like him and finds his ultimate identity in the eyes of his creator. It's a good story, and believe it or not, your guys will likely listen attentively.

After you read the book, have them explain how this story relates to what you've been talking about in this session.

Give your guys a high five, go over the **Soul Work** assignment, and close in prayer, asking God to remind each of you of your value and identity this week.

Super Bonus Points: Bring in someone else to share a story from his life: A retired gentleman, an ex-pro athlete, or someone else who has experienced a loss of identity before.

Option Three: War Story

This idea of getting your identity, value, and self-worth from God instead of from what the culture says is TOUGH. And it's tough for all of us, especially when it comes to change.

A lot of men feel a real sense of loss or mourning when they retire from their jobs. They've always thought of themselves as the business guy, the money maker, the executive, the breadwinner—and huge parts of their identities are wrapped up in what they've done for careers. And once they retire, they feel put out to pasture.

I know a couple of guys who were great baseball players and tried to make the Major Leagues, but because of one reason or another they had to retire early and never made the bigs. They suffered major depression because they didn't know life outside of being ballplayers.

Share a story from your life or the life of someone you know. Better yet, have someone come in and share from his heart (see box).

Then close it up by saying something like, **When you base your value and self-worth on the things of our culture, the things it says are valuable, you set yourself up for failure. But when you see yourself as God sees you, you can base your identity on that, and it'll transform your life forever.**

Briefly go over the **Soul Work** assignment and close in prayer, asking God to remind each of you of your value and identity this week.

WILL THE REAL SLIM SHADY PLEASE STAND UP?
MEDIA VERSUS REALITY

"See to it that no one takes you captive through hollow and deceptive philosophy, which depends on human tradition and the elemental spiritual forces of this world rather than on Christ." (Colossians 2:8)

(Don't become captured by what someone else thinks you should be—especially when it's based on what culture thinks instead of what God thinks. Here are three other reasons.)

1. Even what you think is reality often is <u>not</u>.

    (Looking at those "before and after" photos makes you wonder how often what's portrayed isn't even real. And you begin basing your feelings and thoughts on things that don't even exist. Yikes!)

2. Don't play the <u>comparison</u> game.

    (You're thinking, "I should look like that"—when it isn't even real. That thinking is hollow and deceptive. If you base your value on what you look like, how big your muscles are, how much money you make, or the car you drive, you'll never be happy. Someone will always be better looking, stronger, faster, make more money, or drive a better car, etc.)

3. Your self-worth should come from your <u>Creator</u>.

    (God made you. God doesn't make junk! You are his creation.)

More from the Bible, God's Word

4. You're created in God's <u>image</u>.

    "So God created human beings in his own image, in the image of God he created them; male and female he created them." (Genesis 1:27)

    (You were made in God's likeness. You aren't an accident. Even if you were an accident in your parents' planning, you weren't an accident in God's planning. God made you, created you, shaped you. Just as a kid takes after his parents, you take after God.)

5. You're a <u>spiritual</u> being.

"But it is the spirit in mortals, the breath of the Almighty, that gives them understanding." (Job 32:8)

(You're not just a bunch of cells and hair. You have a soul, a spirit. Even when your body dies, your spirit will go on living forever. You have the breath of God inside you.)

6. You're <u>priceless</u>.

"For you know that it was not with perishable things such as silver or gold that you were redeemed from the empty way of life handed down to you from your ancestors, but with the precious blood of Christ, a lamb without blemish or defect." (1 Peter 1:18-19)

(You have infinite worth. You were worth God giving his own son for you. I mean, I like you and care about you, but I'm not trading my son for you. But God did! Whoa! Our value comes from the price God put on us—not from what the media says about us, what we should look like, the kinds of clothes we should wear, how big our muscles should be, or what kind of cars we should drive.)

WILL THE REAL SLIM SHADY PLEASE STAND UP?
MEDIA VERSUS REALITY

"See to it that no one takes you captive through hollow and deceptive philosophy, which depends on human tradition and the elemental spiritual forces of this world rather than on Christ." (Colossians 2:8)

1. Even what you think is reality often is n_____.

2. Don't play the c_____ game.

    If you base your value on what you look like, how big your muscles are, how much money you make, or the car you drive, you'll never be happy. Someone will always be better looking, stronger, faster, make more money, or drive a better car, etc.

3. Your self-worth should come from your C_____.

More from the Bible, God's Word

4. You're created in God's i_____.

    "So God created human beings in his own image, in the image of God he created them; male and female he created them." (Genesis 1:27)

5. You're a s_____ being.

    "But it is the spirit in mortals, the breath of the Almighty, that gives them understanding." (Job 32:8)

6. You're p_____.

    "For you know that it was not with perishable things such as silver or gold that you were redeemed from the empty way of life handed down to you from your ancestors, but with the precious blood of Christ, a lamb without blemish or defect." (1 Peter 1:18-19)

SOUL WORK

This week's **Soul Work** is without a doubt the craziest, funniest, and maybe one of the coolest Bible studies ever. We're talking about circumcision. (Ouch, I know. I'm feeling it.) Kind of weird talking about it, but what we're going to discover is key to what being a godly man is all about.

1. Read Genesis 17:1-9 and answer these questions.

    ▷ How old was Abram when God appeared to him?

    ▷ God changes Abram's name to _____.

    ▷ What does his new name mean? F_____ of many n_____.

    ▷ What is God's promise to Abram?

    ▷ Skip ahead to Genesis 22:17-18. How many kids will Abraham have?

2. Okay, back to Genesis 17. Now read verses 10-13.

    ▷ So God's covenant is to give Abraham as many descendants as there are stars in the sky. All Abraham has to do is...what?

Can you imagine what Abraham was feeling and thinking? I imagine him saying, "God, you want me to do WHAT?" I mean, we don't even know if Abraham knew what circumcision was. He might have had to say, "Sure, God. I'll do anything. Can you just tell me what circumcision is?" And then to have to get circumcised at 99 years old—whoa!

In biblical times, if you were going to be a man of God, you had to get circumcised. That's part of what being a man was...but not really. Circumcision set the Jews apart from the other people. God chose them. He made them special. And it was a *daily* reminder of who and whose they were. They were God's. Not their own.

Unfortunately, many men forgot the significance of what circumcision meant. And many men would be circumcised and then live the most ungodly lives. It was as if their bodies were marked for God, but they were living for themselves. Circumcision not only became meaningless, but it became a test of devotion. If you were God's chosen, you had to get circumcised.

But being a man, being a man after God's own heart, isn't about whether you're circumcised or not. Look at what Paul wrote about circumcision.

3. Read 1 Corinthians 7:19.

    ▷ How important is being circumcised or uncircumcised?

    ▷ What really counts in God's eyes?

4. Read Galatians 5:6.

    ▷ How valuable is being circumcised or uncircumcised?

    ▷ The only thing that counts is...what?

5. Read Galatians 6:15.

    ▷ What does it mean to be circumcised or uncircumcised?

    ▷ What really counts?

6. Read 2 Corinthians 5:17.

    ▷ If anyone is in Christ, he is a...what?

    ▷ Do you believe in Jesus Christ?

    ▷ If you believe in Jesus Christ, that makes you a...what?

Nice job. Being a man is about knowing you are God's precious creation. You're loved. And when you experience God's love, Christ's love overflows from your life and into the lives of others.

    You rock! Have a great week!

CHAPTER THREE

EXTREME MAKEOVER, GUYS' EDITION: BEING A CHILD OF THE KING

THE BIG IDEA

You are a child of the King.

Main Text

> "If you belong to Christ, then you are Abraham's seed, and heirs according to the promise." (Galatians 3:29)

What's the Point?

Knowing who and whose I am radically shapes my identity. When students know they're children of the King, heirs with Jesus, God's sons, then they're free to live without masks. Then it's okay not to be okay. Everything doesn't have to be all right. Finally, some great men of the Bible were able to step out from their masks and still be REAL men.

RECAP SOUL WORK

Hopefully, you didn't get too many phone calls or complaints about sending your guys home with a Bible study about circumcision.

If your guys are anything like mine, they probably left their **Soul Work** sheets in their Bibles at the gym. Middle schoolers! But if your guys have done the **Soul Work**, reward them. Tell them they did a great job and that it takes real men to finish assignments.

Whether they completed the sheets or not, briefly go over the main points, which are:

1. **In the old days, people looked on the outside to see if you belonged to God. You were marked.**

2. **Once Jesus came, the mark became harder to see since it was marked on your heart instead of on your body.**

3. **Being a man is about knowing and understanding God's love for you, which is part of what we're talking about today.**

Wrap up with a word of prayer and head on to the **Opening Activity**.

OPENING ACTIVITY
Option One: Guess the King Quiz

Tell your guys you want to begin this week by talking about royalty. Say something like, **Gentlemen, today we're going to test your knowledge of royalty and see if you can spot royalty when you see it.**

Give them the instructions for the quiz or use PowerPoint and have them go through it. Make sure to award the winner(s) a sweet prize, such as a candy bar, a ticket to a movie, a can of soda, a double high five, the keys to your new Lincoln Navigator, etc.

After they finish the quiz, try to bring some meaning to the quiz by asking some of the following questions.

1. **What do you think it's like to be a king? What's a king's life like?** (*Possible answers: Kings are so rich; they have people bowing down to them; maybe their faces are on their countries' money; stressful; they have boats, swimming pools, more money than they know what to do with.*)

2. **What kinds of privileges do people of royalty get?** (*Everything's free. They can do and say whatever they want. They get only the best food and drinks, clothes, cars, houses, etc.*)

3. **Think of some of the people in the quiz. What do you imagine life is like for them?** (*They're spoiled, rich. They can get whatever they want, whenever they want, however they want, etc. They have lots of "friends" because they have lots of money.*)

4. **Now imagine the children of "royalty." What do you think life is like for those kids?** (*The best life ever! They would get whatever they wanted—the best toys, games, etc. Paris Hilton is one of those kids. When her parents die, she's one of the main heirs or receivers of the inheritance. Whoa!*)

YOU'LL NEED

Guess the King Quiz handout (or create a PowerPoint version of the game) and some sweet prizes for the winners of the quiz; construction equipment, such as a hammer, tool belt, tape measure; a few minutes taped from one of the *Extreme Makeover: Home Edition* shows; various tools; some funky old-school beats for a rap, a cap worn to the side, a big gold necklace, some shades, and your Adidas (all to use in the rap option); *Powder* DVD; enough Burger King crowns for your students; markers; Beth Moore's book, *A Parable About the King*

GUESS THE KING ANSWERS

Queen Elizabeth
Burger King
King James (LeBron James)
Queen Amidala
BB King
Paris Hilton
Prince Charles
The Princess
Dr. Martin Luther King, Jr.
The King, Elvis Aaron Presley

Now transition to the **Big Picture** by saying something like this: **The Bible says we—you and I—are sons of a King as well. Let's talk about what that means.**

Option Two: Extreme Makeover

We want to start getting guys thinking again about changing their ideas of what a real man is supposed to be. So we're going to try to relate it to something abstract: Extreme makeovers. See the sidebar for more on teaching abstract ideas to middle school guys.

Play your taped *Extreme Makeover: Home Edition* clip for an intro. If you don't have a clip, no sweat—talk about the show. Most students are familiar with it. If you have any tools you can bring in and talk about building stuff, those will be a huge help, too.

Here are some questions to help the conversation:

▷ **Have you ever seen one of those makeover shows, such as *Extreme Makeover: Home Edition*?**

▷ **Have you ever been involved in rebuilding something?**

▷ **When someone wants to make over their house or car, what does he want to do?** *(Change it, make it better, etc.)*

▷ **What has to happen first? How would he begin the makeover?** *(You'll probably get a wide array of answers here, but try to direct them to the idea of tearing out the old, problem stuff before they can put in the new, good stuff.)*

Then say something like, **Today we're going to try to do an extreme makeover with you guys. No, we won't be putting on makeup or doing your hair. But we want to do some deconstruction, as we've been doing the past few weeks. And we want to build some new identity in you. And we'll begin by talking about who you really are.**

Option Three: War Story

Feel free to use some of the stuff in **Option Two** about those makeover shows and introduce the idea that way. Then take time to share a story in your life when you did your own "extreme makeover."

Maybe you rebuilt a car. Maybe you had to drywall the basement. Better yet, maybe you remember working with your dad on a huge project. Maybe you put a new roof on your house or had to resod the lawn.

Talk about the fun of breaking down walls. Grab your hammer and share about the pain of carrying materials across the yard, down the stairs, etc. And the creation of something new and how great that was, the feeling almost of disbelief as you looked at what you'd accomplished.

Here's where you'll need to make the rough abstract transition.

Tell them, **Today we're going to keep demolishing some of those bad ideas about what a real man is. One idea in particular is the mask of the boy code we've talked about—that idea of no matter what, we have to pretend everything's just fine. We can't cry or else we're weak or "girly."**

Continue, **Those kinds of lame ideas need to go. And hopefully, we're going to tear them out today and build something solid in their place. We're going to take a look at some guys in the Bible who were awesome men, so let's jump in.**

THE BIG PICTURE

The big idea we want to get across is, when you know who you are, when you know you're God's son, you're free to take off the mask, to stop pretending everything's just fine. The only accepted feeling guys aren't ridiculed for is anger. And when you know who you are, you're free to get angry. But you don't have to allow yourself to be straitjacketed into only that one feeling.

We'll take a look at two real men, King David and Jesus, and see how they both knew who they were. And because they knew, they were free to feel anger and sadness—and other emotions. For them it was okay not to be okay.

Then we'll direct the guys back to themselves, and hopefully, something amazing will take place. Hopefully, they'll dig into God's Word and see for the very first time that they are, in fact, sons of God. They're heirs. Princes. And if they can catch on to this idea, if they can see their self-worth through God's lenses, maybe we'll help free them from the yoke of slavery—the mask.

For a lot of our guys, this idea of abstract thinking, is, well, abstract. To have them try to relate tearing down a house and rebuilding it to tearing down our old ideas about what a man is and rebuilding them may be a bit much, especially if you have sixth-graders.

The more concrete things you have to help communicate the idea, the better off you'll be.

Be patient. These kids play tons of video games, so they can and do think abstractly. The real-world stuff is just a little difficult sometimes.

Dig into the **Outline** together. You can either let your guys work on their own and then get together to go over the answers, or you can do it all together. After you're done, proceed to the **Breakdown**.

BREAKDOWN

Option One: Email Mark

Read your guys the following blog entry from a student named Mark.

> **My dad has cancer. AGAIN. I found out a few months ago. He already had it once and he beat it. But I guess it's back. People at church know because he's on the prayer list. People have asked me how it's going and how I am, but I don't want to talk about it. I just tell them, "I'm fine." Or, "Everything's okay." But it's not. I'm scared, but I don't want people to think I'm a wimp. I mean, I don't want to lose my dad. I'm supposed to be tough. My dad told me, "Be strong. Don't cry." But that's all I want to do. Cry.**

Tell your guys to pretend they know Mark and have each student write Mark an encouraging note and maybe some advice on how to deal with his feelings.

After your students are done writing (and you've wrestled down the sixth-grader who keeps throwing pencils across the room), have each one of the students share his response.

Once they're done, encourage them about their responses and transition to the **Closing Activity** by saying something like, **Sometimes it can be so hard to be real and share your feelings. But when you know who you are, when you know you're God's son, a child of the King, it makes it easier to share those feelings, knowing you're even manlier than someone who's afraid. Great job, guys!**

Option Two: Word Up! Write a Rap

Anytime you can get students to process what you're teaching them in a fun and creative way, it's a win-win situation. So try to get your guys to process what we learned on the **Outline** by making up a rap. Yup, it's hokey—I admit it. But with a little energy and a good attitude (and your "rap outfit"), you could make it really fun and memorable.

Have your guys write raps about what we're talking about. The verses don't have to be long. If they end up with limericks or funny nursery rhymes, then they still win.

If you make up your own and perform it before the guys begin working on theirs, they'll have a better idea of what you're looking for. If you can't make up any lyrics, just rap the following ones:

Yo! Yo! Yo! Yo! Yo! Yo! Yo!

I got some news that you need to KNOW.

Sometimes it's hard to be a MAN.

No one really underSTANDS.

When a dude is hurting, he can't CRY;

He's got to be tough, he's got to TRY.

But every man has got some TEARS

From all the pain throughout the YEARS.

So it's good to be a child of the KING

Where it's safe to hurt when life STINGS.

When you know WHO you are, it's safe to BE

A real man who don't hide his FEELINGS.

Word!

Oh my, that is bad (and not bad in a good way). Let them laugh and have fun and help them process this idea. Then have them read or perform their masterpieces.

Finally, wrap up this part of the session by saying, **Making up a rap may seem silly, hokey, or lame. But knowing who you are—knowing you're a child of the King—is powerful.**

HOKEY ALERT

Sometimes the things we do can be so hokey. And if you try to pass them off as being cool, your guys will see right through you.

But if you call it hokey from the beginning and have fun and a good attitude, sometimes you can take something hokey and make it a great memorable moment.

Option Three: Movie Clip

The movie *Powder* is about a young teenager named Jeremy who has ghost-like pale skin (thus the nickname "Powder") and evidently can't grow hair. His grandfather lets him out of the house and has him go to school, and Jeremy has to deal with the everyday ridicule you'd expect—except for one thing. Jeremy has some strange powers, including the ability to look into people's hearts.

Set up the clip by saying, **Knowing that real men such as David and Jesus were not only angry sometimes, but also able to express emotion and even cry is really powerful. For some of us showing emotions is really difficult because if we're going to cry, we have to let our guard down. We have to admit we're weak. And we'd rather hide our emotions behind a mask.**

Tell the students you want to show them a clip from a movie called *Powder*. Tell them the back story, play the clip (start 1:26:00, a town carnival; stop 1:30:59, Jeremy and Lindsey kiss), and go through the questions that follow.

  ▷ **Do you agree or disagree with Jeremy when he says disconnection and separation are feelings we're taught and we shouldn't have to lie or hide emotions? Why?**

  ▷ **What happens when Lindsey touches his hand?**

  ▷ **What do you think would happen if we could all look inside each other? What if we could see behind everyone's masks?**

  ▷ **Why were David and Jesus able to live without wearing masks?** *(Because they knew who they were. Their self-worth, their confidence, came from being children of the King.)*

  ▷ **What do you think is tougher—wearing a mask and hiding your feelings or being real with your feelings and risking being made fun of? Why?**

Transition to the last section by saying something like, **Isn't it great to know you don't have to hide behind a mask? Let's talk more about what it means to be a child of the King.**

CLOSING ACTIVITY

Option One: Burger King Crowns

Have your students open up their Bibles to 1 Peter 2:9. It says, "But you are a chosen people, a royal priesthood, a holy nation, God's special possession, that you may declare the praises of him who called you out of darkness into his wonderful light."

Read the Scripture out loud together and talk about what it means to be a "chosen people," a "holy nation," and people belonging to God.

When you're done, give each student a Burger King crown. Have the students write the 1 Peter verse out on their crowns or paper or hands, etc., to remind them they belong to God and they're children of God, princes in God's Kingdom.

Then have them wear their crowns as you close in prayer and go over this week's **Soul Work** assignment.

Option Two: *A Parable About the King*

This is a great story about the unconditional love of God and a princess who disguises herself because she wants to join what everyone else is doing.

Now none of your guys are princesses. But the story can ring true for them as well. In a world where we often look at other people and want to be just like them, cool like them, dressed like them, etc., this book is a reminder of who we are.

Read through the story and relate it to what you've been talking about and how knowing you're a child of the King radically changes how you live your life. Once you're done, pray together and go over this week's **Soul Work** assignment.

Option Three: "The President and the Little Boy"[2]

Share this story:

> **During the Civil War, a young soldier in the Union Army lost his older brother and father in the battle of Gettysburg. The soldier decid-**

[2] Rice, Wayne. *Hot Illustrations for Youth Talks* on CD-ROM Version 1.0. Grand Rapids, MI: Zondervan, 2001.

NO BK? NO TIME? NO PROBLEM

Hey, if you don't have a Burger King or don't have time to run to one, you can do this exercise on the guys' hands, on tape, on sticky notes, on shoes, on their foreheads (Deuteronomy 11:18), etc. Be creative.

ed to go to Washington, D.C., to see President Lincoln to ask for an exemption from military service so he could go back home and help his sister and mother. When he arrived in Washington, after having received time off from the military to plead his case, he went to the White House and asked to see the President.

The guard on duty told him, "You can't see the President! Don't you know there's a war going on? The President is a very busy man. Now go away! Get back out there on the battle lines where you belong."

So the young soldier left, very disheartened, and was sitting on a park bench not far from the White House when a little boy came up to him. The boy said, "Soldier, you look unhappy. What's wrong?" The soldier looked at the little boy and began to tell his story. The little boy listened and said, "I can help you, soldier." He took the soldier by the hand and led him back to the front gate of the White House. Apparently, the guard didn't notice them because they weren't stopped. They walked straight to the front door of the White House and walked right in. After they got inside, they walked right past generals and high-ranking officials, and no one said a word. The soldier couldn't understand this. Why didn't anyone try to stop them?

Finally, they reached the Oval Office—where the President was working—and the little boy didn't even knock on the door. He just walked right in and led the soldier in with him. There behind the desk was Abraham Lincoln and his Secretary of State, looking over battle plans laid out on his desk.

The President looked at the boy and then at the soldier and said, "Good afternoon, Todd. Can you introduce me to your friend?"

And Todd Lincoln, the son of the President, said, "Daddy, this soldier needs to talk to you."

The soldier pled his case before Mr. Lincoln, and right then and there he received the exemption he desired.

Where to take it from here: **Because Jesus Christ died for us, we're God's sons, and we have direct access to God.**

After you share this story, pray with your guys and go over this week's **Soul Work** assignment.

EXTREME MAKEOVER, GUYS' EDITION: BEING A CHILD OF THE KING

(Before we can go on, we need to cover...)

One big question: <u>Who are you</u>?

*(Yes, you're [**NAME**]. And yes, you are your parents' kid. But you're something greater yet.)*

"If you belong to Christ, then you are Abraham's seed, and heirs according to the promise." (Galatians 3:29)

Congratulations! You're rich. This verse says if you belong to Christ, you're an heir. If you belong to Christ (which means, if you believe in Jesus), then you've just inherited a HUGE fortune.

You see, when you know who you are, you're free to take off the mask and experience the great life God has for us.

(Next have them bust out their Bibles and go through the rest of the Outline, filling in the blanks.)

The man's name	Who is he?	What does he feel?
King David	A man after God's own <u>heart</u> (1 Samuel 13:14) *(Saul is rejected as king, and God is talking about David.)*	<u>anger at God</u> (2 Samuel 6:8) *(God kills Uzzah for disobeying, and David's angry about it.)* <u>sadness, weeping</u> (1 Samuel 30:3-4) *(David's wives and children have been captured.)*
The King of Kings, Jesus	God's <u>Son</u> (John 3:16) *(Jesus is the real deal, God's Son.)*	<u>anger at people</u> (Matthew 21:12) *(They have turned the temple into a flea market and are exploiting people.)* <u>weeping, sadness, depression</u> (John 11:35) *(Jesus' good friend Lazarus dies.)*
Prince _____ (Insert your name here.)	I'm also God's <u>son</u>. (Romans 8:16-17, Galatians 4:4-7) *(Because of Jesus, I'm a son. Because I'm a son, I'm also an heir.)*	"A <u>sad face</u> is good for the heart." (Ecclesiastes 7:3) *(It's good to be real. Don't hide behind the mask. You're safe.)* "In your anger do <u>not sin</u>." (Ephesians 4:26) *(There's nothing wrong with being angry. But don't let it control you.)*

GUESS THE KING QUIZ

Rules: Fight it out in this royal guessing game as you battle your fellow squires to discover who each of these "kings" and "queens" is.

Example: "Second verse, same as the first!" He had two of his wives beheaded. Don't get on this king's bad side. Answer: King Henry VIII

1. Windsor + bad teeth + corgis + long version of "Beth" =

2. Hold the pickle, hold the lettuce—have it your way at...

3. This guy became a pro basketball star straight out of high school. What's his nickname?

4. In a galaxy far, far away...

5. His guitar's name was Lucille, and oh, could he make her sing—especially the blues.

6. She's the heiress of a famous hotel family.

7. Well, he may never be king, but he IS royalty. Was once married to Lady Diana...

8. Koopa had her captured in the castle, and Mario and Luigi had to find her.

9. We celebrate this civil rights hero's birthday every January.

10. The king of rock 'n' roll.

EXTREME MAKEOVER, GUYS' EDITION: BEING A CHILD OF THE KING

One Big Question: _____?

"If you belong to Christ, then you are Abraham's seed, and heirs according to the promise." (Galatians 3:29)

Congratulations! You're rich. This verse says if you belong to Christ, you're an heir. If you belong to Christ (which means, if you believe in Jesus), then you've just inherited a HUGE fortune.

You see, when you know who you are, you're free to take off the mask and experience the great life God has for us.

Grab a Bible and look up the verses to fill in the blanks in this chart.

The man's name	Who is he?	What does he feel?
King David	A man after God's own h_____ (1 Samuel 13:14)	_____ (2 Samuel 6:8) _____ (1 Samuel 30:3-4)
The King of Kings, Jesus	God's _____ (John 3:16)	_____ (Matthew 21:12) _____ (John 11:35)
Prince _____ (Insert your name here.)	I'm also God's _____. (Romans 8:16-17, Galatians 4:4-7)	"A _____ is good for the heart." (Ecclesiastes 7:3) "In your anger do _____." (Ephesians 4:26)

SOUL WORK

This week there are two parts to your **Soul Work.** Let's get to it!

PART ONE

Call up your grandpa and ask him the following questions. Make sure to write down what he says. (If you don't have a grandpa, you can ask another grandpa-type guy, your dad, or any other man you respect.)

1. Tell me about a time when you had to ask for forgiveness from someone. Was it difficult?

2. How did you know you were really forgiven?

3. Can you tell me about a time when you experienced God or felt as if God really loved you?

4. In our group we're talking about what it means to be a man. In your opinion what does it mean to be a real man?

PART TWO

Memorize these two verses from the Bible.

"Whoever does not love does not know God, because God is love." (1 John 4:8)

"As far as sunrise is from sunset, he has separated us from ours sins." (Psalm 103:12, MSG)

CHAPTER FOUR

IDENTITY, PART ONE: YOU ARE LOVED BY GOD AND FORGIVEN FOREVER

THE BIG IDEA

God loves your guys. Period.

Main Text

> "Whoever does not love does not know God, because God is love." (1 John 4:8)

What's the Point?

Now that we've spent the first three sessions deconstructing our guys' identities, it's time to begin building them back up with a godly foundation. Guys must understand that as Christians they're loved and precious to God, and their sins have been forgiven forever. God's love isn't based on their good behavior. God loves them because it's God's nature to love—and, as Christians, the penalty for their sins has been paid in full. They've been forgiven for every sin they've ever done and will do in the future.

RECAP SOUL WORK

Last week's **Soul Work** was two-fold. Have your guys talk about their interviews with their grandfather-type people and share what they discovered. Then have the guys recite their memory verses. Ask them, **What do these verses mean to you? Why do you think they're important?**

(Remember—most likely you're just priming their minds for later, so don't be surprised if you get silence or a bunch of "I dunno" or "Huh?"; and if you're lucky, someone will have burped by now.) Give each guy who memorized the verses a prize of some sort—even if it's a just a high-five. As long as your guys know you're proud of them, you've succeeded.

Transition to the **Opening Activity** by telling them, **Now that you've memorized 1 John 4:8, we're going to spend some time talking about what God's love really means. Let's jump in!**

OPENING ACTIVITY

Option One: Superhero Game

Check out Super Secret Identities at the end of this chapter. This quick quiz focuses on superheroes' secret identities. Here's an example:

Superman is really...A) Regis Philbin, B) Clark Kant, C) Clark Kent, or D) [insert your name here].

Have the students take the quiz and determine your winner. Then say, **We've talked so much about what the world thinks makes a man. Today we're going to focus on the secret identity of a man after God's own heart. A guy needs to know some certain things about his soul. We're gonna hit two core issues today. But first let's pray for our time together.**

Open up in prayer and move on to the **Big Picture**.

Answers for Super Secret Identities and Back Snatchers (Opening Activity, Option Three)

Superman: Clark Kent	Supergirl: Kara Kent
Batman: Bruce Wayne	Batgirl: Barbara Gordon
Robin: Dick Grayson	Catwoman: Selina Kyle
Zorro: Don Diego de la Vega	The Lone Ranger: John Reid
Wonder Woman: Diana Prince	Spider-Man: Peter Parker
The Green Lantern: Alan Scott	

The original Power Rangers: Billy Cranston, Kimberly Hart, Trini Kwan, Jason Lee Scott, Tommy Oliver, and Zack Taylor

Option Two: Your Favorite Superhero Movie

I know you have a favorite superhero movie. Whether it's *Conan*, *Batman*, or *Zorro* or the TV show *The Greatest American Hero*, I know you can find a short two- to three-minute clip of your dude in action.

Share the clip with your guys and tell them why this hero is so cool to you. Then say something to relate his secret identity to the secret identities of our students, such as, **All superheroes, including my favorite, have secret identities. They use these to hide their super powers.**

Go on, **And as we've been discussing, we use masks to hide our real identities. Today we want to start rebuilding those identities and getting an idea of what a godly man feels in the depths of his soul. We're going to go over two core soul feelings today and the rest next week.**

Then have one of the guys or yourself open up in prayer and move on to the **Big Picture.**

Option Three: Back Snatchers

This is a twist on a classic youth ministry game. Print out the **Back Snatchers** handout and cut the secret identities' names into strips, one name per strip. If you have more than 12 boys, you really don't have a small group anymore, so it's okay to make some more of your own sheets or just double them up.

As each guy comes in, tape his secret identity name on his back. It doesn't really matter if he knows who it is or not. Then have the guys take places against the far wall. You don't want them to see the other guys' names yet. Hand each guy a pencil and a sheet of paper.

The object of the game: Be the first guy to get everyone's secret identities on your list. Tell the guys, **Try not to let anyone see your name—that way you increase your chance at fame and fortune and winning this game.** For an easy twist you can also have guys just guess the superhero names and super powers.

After your pastor comes in to shut down the game because you're being too loud, or one of your boys successfully gets all the names down, declare a winner and say, **Each one of these superheroes has a secret identity. We've been hitting the idea of identity really hard these last few weeks, trying to break away from what our culture says makes a real man. Today we're going to start rebuilding a founda-**

tion of what a godly man is and what he feels in the depths of his soul. Let's get started.

Have the winner of the game open you up in prayer and move on to the **Big Picture.**

THE BIG PICTURE

Hold up your flower with many petals and share a story of your middle school days when you were in love with some girl and you did the age-old practice of "she loves me; she loves me not." Pluck the petals away as you tell the story.

Then relate the kind of love you had for the girl to how you sometimes feel with God—as if he loves you when you do good things and "loves you not" when you misbehave.

If I were talking, I'd say something like, **A lot of times I've felt this is how God loves me. Whenever I was reading my Bible, praying, not sinning, etc., I felt as though God loved me. But whenever I was telling dirty jokes or checking out my brother's magazine collection, I felt God didn't love me.**

Continue, **In fact, I was so confident of this, I thought if God returned to earth, and I was in the middle of sinning, he'd send me to hell. I was so scared!**

Now hand out this week's **Outline** and go through it together. Once you finish going over the **Outline**, lead in to the **Breakdown** by restating the **Big Picture: The big idea I want you to get today is, God loves you incredibly and has forgiven you forever. Let's talk a little more about what this really means for us.**

LEADER NOTE: FORGIVENESS

In the **Big Picture** my hope is that you'll teach your guys God has forgiven us for every sin, for all time. Now that sounds nice and all, but most people don't believe it. Sometimes we fear if we teach people God has forgiven them for all their sins now and in the future because the price has already been paid by Jesus, well then, why will people behave? In short, *why will they choose not to sin?*

The alternative is believing you have to ask for forgiveness for every sin you commit without fail or it remains a debit to your account. And not only

Bring in some bricks or cement blocks to help illustrate creating a new foundation.

Talk about the need for a strong foundation, and with each point you share on the **Outline**, get out a brick or block with the idea written on it.

do you have to ask for forgiveness, but you also have to feel really badly about it and really mean it and promise you'll never do it again, etc.

Just a couple thoughts here—

1. There's only one verse in the Bible that comes close to indicating this—1 John 1:9, where John says, "If we confess our sins, he is faithful and just and will forgive us our sins and purify us from all unrighteousness."

Obviously, this book isn't a forum for discussing theological differences, but I encourage you to take seriously the context of 1 John, including verse 8, where John writes, "If we claim to be without sin, we deceive ourselves and the truth is not in us."

John wrote this letter to gnostics who didn't believe in sin. If they would admit they did sin, they would've been admitting their need for a savior. I believe this verse is misinterpreted all the time, and understanding that God has forgiven you for every sin, whether you've remembered to confess it or not, is a radically transforming concept and evidence of the grace of God and God's love.

2. Romans 6:9-10 states, "For we know that since Christ was raised from the dead, he cannot die again; death no longer has mastery over him. The death he died, he died to sin once for all; but the life he lives, he lives to God." Surely Jesus doesn't have to die for our sins every time we sin or confess.

3. I am in no way advocating against confession of sins! Confessing our sins is healthy, and James says, "Therefore confess your sins to each other and pray for each other so that you may be healed" (5:16). I talk a lot about confession and accountability in *Living as a Young Man of God*, the next course book.

4. If you aren't ready to embrace the concept of your sins past, present, and future having been forgiven forever, please communicate to your boys at the very least that God loves them and forgives them of their sins.

BREAKDOWN
Option One: Nail Their Sins to a Cross

Break down your teaching and help your students experience God's forgiveness and grace by nailing their sins to a cross. Give each student a small piece of paper and have each guy write his worst sin, or any sin, on it. If any guy is too embarrassed to write out his sin, he can just make a little symbol on the paper to stand for the sin. No one's going to see the paper, but this might make anyone who's embarrassed feel safer.

Then have the guys go up one at a time and nail the sin papers to the wooden cross with a hammer. You have a few options once the students are done: Leave the cross in its spot as a visual reminder of Christ paying for our sins or take off the pieces of paper and throw them away to demonstrate the sins being gone.

Whichever you do, transition to the **Closing Activity** by saying, **Isn't it great to know and feel God's forgiveness? I have one more thing to share with you before we go.**

Option Two: Grilling—Old Testament Versus New Testament

In the **Big Picture** we talked about God's love and complete forgiveness. Sometimes it's still difficult to understand why and how God has forgiven us. The students need to understand that Jesus is and was the ultimate sacrifice. Without boring your guys, you need to help them understand the Old Testament way of paying for sins and how Jesus is the ultimate fulfillment of that.

One way to get the point across is to act out a scene with some action figures. For example, you can have Batman and G.I. Joe sinning, feeling bad, finding a cat, symbolically placing their sins on the cat, and then cooking the cat on a toy grill. Note: This addition to the session is pretty easy if you have kids at home. If you don't, head down to Goodwill for some cheap toys.

You can explain by saying something like, **In Old Testament times when people sinned, they would have to sacrifice animals to pay the penalty for their sins. Death was the penalty for sinning. Blood had to spill. Either *you* could die for your sins, or you could symbolically place your sins on a helpless animal and then kill the animal. Something had to die, and most people preferred to let the animals die.**

Now say, **When Jesus came, because he lived a life without one sin, he was the perfect and sinless sacrifice. And when he died, he paid the debt for every sin anyone ever committed or will commit.**

Have the guys open their Bibles to Ephesians 1:7 and say, **In *The Message* this verse reads, "Because of the sacrifice of the Messiah, his blood poured out on the altar of the Cross, we're a free people— free of penalties and punishments chalked up by all our misdeeds.**

And not just barely free, either. Abundantly free!" Also, Hebrews 9:26 says, "[Christ] has appeared once for all at the culmination of the ages to do away with sin by the sacrifice of himself."

Briefly go over the meanings of those verses if you haven't already and remind them again: **God loves us so much, he gave his one and only Son, and if we believe in Jesus, we'll receive everlasting life. Whoa!** Then head on to the **Closing Activity.**

CLOSING ACTIVITY
Option One: "A Vision of Jesus"[3]

Tell your students, **Author and speaker Brennan Manning tells the story of a woman who visited her priest and told him that when she prays, she sees Jesus in a vision.** Then read them the story.

> "He appears to me as real as you are standing here right now, Father," said the woman. "And he speaks to me. He tells me he loves me and wants to be with me. Do you think I'm crazy?"
>
> "Not at all," replied the priest. "But to make sure it is really Jesus who's visiting you, I want you to ask him a question when he appears to you again. Ask him to tell you the sins I confessed to him in confession. Then come back and tell me what he said."
>
> A few days later the woman returned.
>
> "Did you have another vision of Jesus?" the priest inquired of her.
>
> "Yes, I did, Father," she replied.
>
> "And did you ask him to tell you the sins I confessed to him while I was in confession?"
>
> "Yes, I did," the woman answered.
>
> "And what did he tell you?" asked the priest expectantly.
>
> "He said...'I forgot.'"

[3] Brennan Manning, *The Ragamuffin Gospel: Embracing the Unconditional Love of God* (Multnomah, 1990) 116-117.

Now say, **Jesus graciously forgives and forgets our sins. Scripture assures us of this: "I, even I, am he who blots out your transgressions…and remembers your sins no more," says God (Isaiah 43:25).**

Pray over the guys and bless them, touching each one of them on the shoulder or head, if you feel comfortable doing so. When you finish, distribute this week's **Soul Work** handout.

Option Two: Picture in Your Wallet

Pull out your wallet and talk about its contents. Pull out a picture of someone special in your wallet and explain why you keep her picture there (e.g., she's very special; you don't want to forget about her; she always makes you smile, etc.).

Then say something like, **If God had a wallet, your picture would be in there. That's how special you are to God. You're his precious child. His sweet boy. His handsome son. You are a child of the King. And God loves you so much.**

Pray over the guys and bless them, touching each one of them on the shoulder or head, if you feel comfortable doing so. When you finish, distribute this week's **Soul Work** handout.

Option Three: Jesus-Junk Redemption

Give each guy a "pocket cross," a penny with a cross shape cut out of it, or something similar he can carry around in his pocket all week. Encourage your guys to remember God's love and forgiveness every time they feel or take out their pocket crosses or trinkets.

Pray over the guys and bless them, touching each one of them on the shoulder or head, if you feel comfortable doing so. When you finish, distribute this week's **Soul Work** handout.

IDENTITY, PART ONE: YOU ARE LOVED BY GOD AND FORGIVEN FOREVER

The Big Picture: Building Your Foundation

(As you go through the **Outline**, with every point, stack a brick on top of another brick to visually demonstrate a foundation being constructed.)

1. Brick one: You are <u>loved</u> by God.

   A. God can create a rock so big he can't lift it. True or false?

   B. Is there anything God can't do? Yes or no?

   (Yes! He can't lie. He can't sin. But the biggest point we want to express is...)

   C. God cannot NOT <u>love</u> you. It's God's <u>nature</u> to love.

   (It's who God is. He's perfect love.)

   D. Romans 5:8 says Christ loves you even when you <u>sin</u>.

   (That's radical love. Imagine loving a person who's hurting you. Whoa!)

   E. Romans 8:38-39 says <u>nothing</u> can ever separate you from God's <u>love</u>.

   F. God's love is not <u>conditional</u>. That means it doesn't <u>change</u>.

   (God's love doesn't increase or decrease depending on your behavior. He doesn't love you less when you sin, and he doesn't love you more when you pray, read your Bible, are nice to your sister, clean your room, etc. You probably got that idea from your parents or other adults. God's love for you is the same all the time.)

2. Brick two: You are <u>forgiven</u> <u>forever</u>.

    A. Psalm 103:12 says God has totally separated you from your <u>sins</u>.

       (Jesus was the perfect sacrifice and paid the ultimate price for your and my sins. And he has forgiven you for every one of them.)

    B. Jesus died for all of your sins in the <u>past</u>, <u>present</u>, and <u>future</u>.

       (When Jesus died on the cross, he didn't just die for your sins up to today. NO! He died for every one of your sins in the past, for the sins you'll commit today, and for all the sins you'll ever do in the future.)

SUPER SECRET IDENTITIES

Use your superior intellectual strength to match each superhero with his or her secret identity.

Superman	Don Diego de la Vega
Supergirl	Dick Grayson
Batman	Kimberly Hart
Batgirl	Barbara Gordon
Robin	Trini Kwan
Catwoman	Clark Kent
Zorro	Jason Lee Scott
The Lone Ranger	Selina Kyle
The original Power Rangers	Kara Kent
Wonder Woman	Peter Parker
Spider-Man	Zack Taylor
The Green Lantern	Diana Prince
	Billy Cranston
	John Reid
	Alan Scott
	Bruce Wayne
	Tommy Oliver

BACK SNATCHERS

Cut out these names and slap them on the backs of your lucky middle schoolers for **Opening Activity, Option Three.**

Don Diego de la Vega	Jason Lee Scott	Billy Cranston
Dick Grayson	Selina Kyle	John Reid
Kimberly Hart	Kara Kent	Alan Scott
Barbara Gordon	Peter Parker	Bruce Wayne
Trini Kwan	Zack Taylor	Tommy Oliver
Clark Kent	Diana Prince	

IDENTITY, PART ONE: YOU ARE LOVED BY GOD AND FORGIVEN FOREVER

The Big Picture: Building Your Foundation

1. Brick one: You are l_____ by God.

    A. God can create a rock so big he can't lift it. True or false? (Circle one.)

    B. Is there anything God can't do? Yes or no? (Circle one.)

    C. God cannot NOT l_____ you. It's God's n_____ to love.

    D. Romans 5:8 says Christ loves you even when you _____.

    E. Romans 8:38-39 says _____ can ever separate you from God's l_____.

    F. God's love is not _____. That means it doesn't _____.

2. Brick two: You are f_____ f_____.

    A. Psalm 103:12 says God has totally separated you from your _____.

    B. Jesus died for all of your sins in the p_____, p_____, and f_____.

SOUL WORK

CATERPILLAR RESEARCH

All right guys, your **Soul Work** assignment for this week is to do some quick research with your dad or mom about caterpillars. Answer these three questions to get ready for our session next week.

1. What does the word *chrysalis* mean?

2. Describe how caterpillars get out of their cocoons.

3. How do caterpillars and butterflies and the chrysalis process relate to becoming a Christian?

CHAPTER FIVE

IDENTITY, PART TWO: YOU ARE A NEW CREATION, HOLY AND FREE

THE BIG IDEA

You are a new creation, holy and free.

Main Text

> Once you were alienated from God and were enemies in your minds because of your evil behavior. But now he has reconciled you by Christ's physical body through death to present you holy in his sight, without blemish and free from accusation. (Colossians 1:21-22)

What's the Point?

In the previous session we began helping our guys form new identities in Jesus and took some huge strides as we encouraged them to see that they're loved by God and forgiven forever. The characteristics discussed in this chapter again form foundational beliefs, and if our guys can grasp these beliefs, they'll radically change who they are.

Today you'll help the guys understand that when they decide to follow Jesus, they become new creations. These new creations aren't just middle school guys, but holy, set apart—sacraments if you will. And as holy people, they can understand and appreciate the freedom they have in Christ Jesus.

Before You Begin

You'll want to create an air of curiosity in your room. Before you begin, hide something ordinary under a black blanket and put your "Keep out"-type sign on it. Or put a similar sign on a closed door.

Either way, you want to draw interest to one of these two items. You want guys wondering what's behind the door or under the cloth. You don't need to worry about explaining anything just yet.

Simply make a side comment as you begin, such as, **I'm glad you all made it; it's good to see you—and please don't open that door. Don't even worry about the door. Let's get started.**

Do whatever you can to keep the guys' interest in the door or blanket for a bit but don't let them see what's behind the door or underneath the cloth. They'll have plenty of opportunity to discover what you're hiding later.

YOU'LL NEED

Something ordinary to hide; a black blanket; a sign saying something like, "Don't uncover," "Don't look underneath," "Danger," "Keep out," "Warning," or "Don't open this door"; something sort of semisacred from your house; some play dough; a prize; cool-looking butterfly stickers or a marker to draw on the guys' hands; some kind of cool and inexpensive bracelets or necklaces for your guys (if you can't find any, you can make some out of leather and some beads from a craft store)

RECAP SOUL WORK

In last week's **Soul Work** we had a super mini-caterpillar research project. In case the guys forgot it, lost it, or had to update their blogs instead of doing the **Soul Work**, you may need to go over the idea of what the chrysalis process is and relate it to becoming a Christian.

Here's the short version: **Before a caterpillar becomes a butterfly, it goes through a process in which it encapsulates itself into a tight silk cocoon. After a set time the caterpillar slowly squeezes itself out of a hole and emerges a transformed creature. It changes from being a dirt-eating, crawling-on-its-stomach bug to a beautiful butterfly sought after and admired by all. It's a new creation.**

Continue, **You don't see butterflies acting like caterpillars. They don't crawl on the ground anymore. They can't! Instead they fly. They soar. It's the same with us. When we follow Jesus, we aren't the same as we once were. We don't do the same things; we don't act the same way. Unfortunately, many of us forget we're new creations.**

By now your guys should have tears streaming down their cheeks. They should be rending their clothes and preparing to believe in Jesus right there. Okay...maybe not. Just hit the main points of the process. You'll most likely come back to the idea of the chrysalis at the conclusion.

OPENING ACTIVITY
Option One: Holy, Holy, Holy

We want to introduce the idea of holiness to our guys and begin to get them thinking about what being holy means.

In my house it's pretty easy to know what's "holy." My sweet wife has an autographed NFL football by Hall of Famer Steve Young that's off-limits to everyone. If you have something off-limits, something semi-sacred in your home, bring it in and talk about it. It could be an expensive piece of technology, rare sports memorabilia, the curriculum you're reading right now—you know, anything really valuable....

Use some of the following questions to get the conversation going. (I'll answer them as if I were teaching, but of course, adapt your answers for your sacred object.)

> ▷ **What am I holding?** That's right. This is an autographed football signed by the great Steve Young. I barely escaped the house with this thing, and if Jen knew I brought it here, she'd kill me!

> ▷ **Why is this thing so valuable?** For one thing it's signed by Steve Young, and he's a Hall of Famer. Second, because of his signature, it's worth a lot of money. Third, if I ever lost this, I'd have a hard time getting another one. Fourth, when Steve dies, it'll be worth even more. And lastly, it's 49ers memorabilia, baby. That alone makes it valuable. Okay...maybe not.

> ▷ **How do you think we treat this thing?** With tenderness and care. We don't play with it; we don't touch it, nothing. This thing is set apart. We don't want anyone to mess with it.

> ▷ **How is this thing similar to YOU?** You're both of incredible value. While the ball may really be worth only a few hundred dollars, you're valuable because you're God's creation—priceless. And because of that, you're set apart and holy as well.

> ▷ **What do you think it means to be holy?**

Have the guys share their answers and then move to the next step by saying something like, **Today we're going to talk about what it means to be a new creation and how God has made us holy.** Then have someone pray and ask God to show you what it means to be holy.

Option Two: Something Sacred Story

If you're having trouble coming up with some kind of story about something sacred, whether you're short on time or you just can't find the junior golf trophy you won in second grade when you beat Tiger Woods, don't sweat it.

Just use a fun story about something that was the "holy of holies" in your house. Maybe it was your dad's shop or your mom's sports car. Maybe you had a rare baseball card 'til your mom threw it out or something. If you're still short, steal this abridged version of a story I love to tell. Add in some details and make it your own.

> I was in fourth grade, and my mom took me to some weird Christmas art festival. It was pretty cool. In the middle of the whole thing was a dance floor where people were doing all kinds of festive dances.
>
> All of a sudden, the most amazing-looking girl in the world came up to me and asked me to dance. Sure, she was probably only in seventh grade, and no, I didn't know how to dance, but we went onto the floor anyway.
>
> And after we danced, she leaned over, pressed her soft lips against my premanly cheek, and kissed me. Blushing, I went over to my mom and vowed never to wash my cheek again.

Then say, **Today we're going to talk about how we're all holy and what that means.** Have someone lead you all in prayer and ask God to show you what it really means to be holy.

Option Three: New Creation Contest

Give your guys each a few cans of play dough and tell them they're gonna have a contest. They each have three minutes to come up with a new creation of some sort. Each new creation will be judged on original idea, design, and creativity. Start timing and let the guys go.

When three minutes are up, give the winner a prize and go over the following questions:

▷ **What was the hardest part of creating something new?**

▷ **If you really could invent and create something new, what would it be?**

▷ **The Bible talks about how when we become Christians, we become new creations. What do you think that means?**

Then say, **Today we're going to pick up where we left off last week and talk more about the new identity God gives us. We'll talk about how God has made us into new creations and made us holy and free.**

Move to the **Big Picture** by having someone pray for your time together.

THE BIG PICTURE

The Big Picture focuses on two key elements: God has made us holy through his Son, and we have incredible freedom in Jesus.

We're holy. Most of us don't think of ourselves as holy. Yet God's Word says we're set apart, chosen, and special. When guys understand they're set apart, they discover purpose and identity they never knew before.

We have incredible freedom in Jesus. Most believers live under this lie: "If I really love Jesus, I would do blank and not do blank."

That lie creates behavioral legalism leading to spiritual death instead of the freedom Jesus Christ gives—which leads to life and greater love.

Grab your Bibles, pass out the **Outline**, and jump into the **Outline** by saying something like, **Let's see what God's Word has to say about this idea of being holy.** After you're done, proceed to the **Breakdown**.

BREAKDOWN
Option One: Don't Look in the Closet!

Direct your guys to the forbidden door or thing you covered earlier. Surely they've been bugging you about it. If you don't have a door in your room, and you used a blanket to cover something else, adapt the questions. Walk through the following questions with the guys.

▷ **I told you guys about the door as we got started, and you guys have done a good job not messing with it. What do you guys think is behind the door?**

- ▷ Why are you guys so interested in the door?
- ▷ We've been in this room for a long time, and none of you guys has ever wondered what's behind that door before. Why now?

Read Romans 7:7 together: **"What shall we say, then? Is the law sinful? Certainly not! Nevertheless, I would not have known what sin was had it not been for the law. For I would not have known what coveting really was if the law had not said, 'You shall not covet.'"**

Say, **How does this verse relate to the sign on the door?** After some answers, say, **The sign on the door made us want to see what was behind the door. In the same way, when we hear about something we shouldn't do, we want to do it. Whether out of curiosity or a feeling of missing out, we want to know what we're missing.**

Go on, **What would happen if there were no sign on the door?** After some answers, say, **Nothing. We wouldn't even think about the door. We wouldn't care. We wouldn't think we were missing out on anything. We wouldn't even know about it. Some people might say if a door has something dangerous inside it, not having a warning sign would be dangerous and maybe even deadly.**

Go ahead and take the sign off the door and say, **Just as I'm putting the sign away, when Jesus died, the old law was put away. He took away the old law. He says there's nothing we need to do or not do to get him to love us any more than he does right now.**

Then transition to the last part by saying, **Knowing God loves me no matter what makes me want to live in God's ways and for him even more.**

Option Two: Agree or Disagree

Okay, let's talk. Most churches want to believe this. Most people do believe the idea that nothing's going to make God love them more or less. Except they don't...not really.

Most people think, "If I just don't sin, then God will somehow give me what I need. Or if I pray more or harder, stop overeating, or give more money, then God will bless me more, take care of me more, love me more," etc.

We still have this idea of religious behavior micromanagement. And yet the gospel goes radically beyond that. When students realize they have freedom from any of those manmade, unwritten rules, it draws them closer to Christ—instead of fear of breaking the rules drawing them to sin.

So hit your guys with this list and ask them whether they agree or disagree with each statement to get the conversation going. Have them vote on their feet by going to one wall or another to show whether they agree or not.

1. **Good Christians shouldn't smoke.**

2. **Christians shouldn't drink alcohol.**

3. **Littering is a sin.**

4. **God will love you more if you read your Bible.**

5. **When you sin, God hates you.**

6. **People obey God out of fear.**

7. **I do my chores because I love doing them.**

8. **I would take out the trash even if my parents didn't get mad at me for not doing it.**

9. **R-rated movies are good for my soul.**

10. **There's nothing wrong with copying my friends' CDs and DVDs.**

Have your guys take their seats and ask them these questions:

▷ **The common theme running through these statements is that we have unwritten rules about what Christians aren't supposed to do. What are some of those unwritten rules?** *(Possible answers: Christians can't cuss, lie, cheat, steal, kill, litter, etc.)*

▷ **Do all of these rules make it easier or harder to live as a Christian? Why?** *(Harder because of all sorts of things we can't do.)*

▷ **What would happen if Christians didn't have any rules?** *(Most people believe if there weren't any rules, then people wouldn't behave. People would go and sin like crazy.)*

Go to the door you put the sign on earlier and do the questions, discussion, and transition from **Option One**.

Option Three: Case Study—Kevin

Read the following story about Kevin and go through the questions following the story.

Kevin is a guy about your age who lives with his two parents and one older brother.

Kevin's older brother is different. He has long hair. He likes to wear darker colors. He cusses, which his parents hate. And Kevin has found packs of cigarettes in his brother's room. None of this would be a big deal, except Kevin really looks up to his brother.

It's not the clothes or the long scraggly hair. Or the cussing or smoking. Kevin thinks his brother dresses like a dork and thinks his brother's smoking and cussing are dumb.

It's his relationship with God. Kevin's brother treats everyone he meets with love and respect. He never picks on Kevin. He does his chores without complaining. And every time the offering plate passes by, he throws in at least $5, even when Kevin knows it's all his brother has. He does the same thing with people begging on the street.

It doesn't make sense. When people see Kevin's brother, they have no idea what a great guy he is—all they see is the long hair, dark clothes, and cigarettes. In fact, Kevin's brother seems more Christian than most of the people at church—except for his habits.

▷ **What's so confusing about Kevin's brother?** (*He smokes. Wears dark clothes. Has long hair. He cusses. You'd never guess he's a Christian.*)

▷ **Some people would say good Christians don't wear dark clothes, smoke, cuss, have long hair. What do you think God says about these things?** (*God doesn't love you more if you have short hair, if you don't cuss, or if you don't smoke. God loves you the same. He cares more about you than about your outward appearance or behavior.*)

▷ **Can someone be a Christian and do that stuff?** *(I suppose if someone can be overweight and love Jesus, someone can smoke and love Jesus. Neither one is what God wants for our lives. But he doesn't love us any less because of it or any more if we're thin and smoke-free.)*

▷ **Do Christians need to keep a list of rules like not smoking, cussing, etc.?** *(Yes and no. Jesus died to free us from the law. We can't improve our standing before God. God loves us no matter what. God really gave us only two laws: Love God and love your neighbor. If you do those two things, you'll be set. So the "yes" part is, sometimes maybe smoking, cussing, etc., might upset your "neighbors," those around you. So maybe you'd have to stop doing them to love your neighbors. But the "no" part is that those behaviors don't make God love you less.)*

CLOSING ACTIVITY

Option One: Caterpillars and Butterflies

Grab your Bible and read 1 Corinthians 6:12 out loud: **"'I have the right to do anything,' you say—but not everything is beneficial. 'I have the right to do anything'—but I will not be mastered by anything."**

Briefly talk about what the verse means. Then remind your guys about the process caterpillars undergo to become butterflies from last week's **Soul Work.**

Challenge them by saying something like, **How many of you guys ever see butterflies crawling on the ground as if they're still caterpillars? Yeah, never. I mean, I suppose a butterfly could if it wanted to. But why would it want to? After all, it can fly!**

Now say, **That's how it is for us as men as well. Sure we can crawl around in the dirt and mud and filth. No, I'm not talking about real dirt. But sure, you can sin in all sorts of different ways. You're free. But...why would you want to? When you can fly in the air and feel the wind on your face, why would you want to crawl on the ground and taste the dirt?**

Talk about this issue. Once the conversation begins to draw to a close or you begin running out of time, hand each guy a cool butterfly sticker to remind him of tonight's session.

You may have trouble finding anything other than girly butterfly stickers. So if you don't find suitable stickers, just use a marker and draw butterflies on their hands as reminders. They might like those better anyway (nothing like a temporary tribal butterfly tattoo...).

Hand out this week's **Soul Work**, pray for each of the guys by name, and get out of there.

Option Two: New Creation Reminder

Grab your Bible and read 1 Corinthians 6:12 out loud: **"'I have the right to do anything,' you say—but not everything is beneficial. 'I have the right to do anything'—but I will not be mastered by anything."** Briefly talk about what the verse means.

Next hand out bracelets or necklaces and remind your guys about who and whose they are: **You're future kings. You're preparing to reign in heaven. You're sons of God and created to have a relationship with God. Every time you put on your [bracelet] [necklace], remember who and whose you are.**

Hand out this week's **Soul Work**, pray for each of your guys by name, and send them off to battle.

Option Three: City Dog versus Country Dog

In closing share this story with your guys:

> **Have you ever noticed the difference between a city dog and a country dog? When you take a city dog out to the country, the city dog goes CRAZY. It runs all over the place, digging up stuff, chasing cars, and bothering other animals. It's almost as if it doesn't know what to do with all the freedom. Instead of being stuck in a tiny backyard or inside a house in the city, it's amazed by all the space to roam.**
>
> **A country dog, on the other hand, just hangs out on the porch. It doesn't run all over the place. It's already been there and done that. It's been around and knows the best place is on the master's porch.**

**Even when the city dog comes up to the porch
and tries to get the country dog to come with
him, the country dog is unmoved. He'd rather
be close to the master than go off exploring.**

Where to take it from here: **In 1 Corinthians 6:12 it says, "'I have
the right to do anything,' you say—but not everything is beneficial. 'I have the right to do anything'—but I will not be mastered
by anything."**

Now explain, **Just like the city dog, we can go off and explore
unknown areas. Everything's allowed. Some areas will be full of
fun; other areas will be full of pain. Not everything is beneficial.
But God gives us the freedom to go.**

Then say, **The wise old country dog has seen enough and knows
life is best close to his master. The same goes for us: Life is best
close to THE Master.**

Finally, hand out this week's **Soul Work**, pray for each of your guys
by name, and send them out for another week of exploration.

IDENTITY, PART TWO: YOU ARE A NEW CREATION, HOLY AND FREE

1. You have been made <u>holy</u>.

   A. "Once you were alienated from God and were enemies in your minds because of your evil behavior. But now he has reconciled you by Christ's physical body through death to present you holy in his sight, without blemish and free from accusation." (Colossians 1:21-22)

   (Once you were God's enemy. But Jesus died for you and paid the price for your sins. Because the price for your sins has been paid, you're without sin. And if you're without sin, you're HOLY. Free from blemish. Free from accusation. Satan loves to accuse us of not being good enough, of having too much sin for God to love us. But he's powerless to change God's love for us.)

   B. "It is because of him that you are in Christ Jesus, who has become for us wisdom from God—that is, our righteousness, holiness and redemption." (1 Corinthians 1:30)

   (We're holy not because of anything we do. Far from it! We're only holy because of Jesus. The fundamental problem for most Christians is our inability to grasp our sacredness. The biggest stumbling block is that we don't understand we're holy. That misunderstanding leads to either guilt [because we aren't like Mother Teresa] or more sin [the normal thing sinners do].

   *Illustration: Ask the students what would happen if the President were to come to town and ask to use a parent's car. Then ask, **How would your parents tell you to treat the car? What will they do to get ready for the President? Why?***

   Of course the parents are going to treat the car as sacred and special. Relate that to our lives and how God wants to use us. Talk about how we should feel about ourselves and how we should prepare for God to use us. Then share with them the new identity in 1C.)

   C. You are one in whom <u>Christ</u> dwells. You are <u>sacred</u> and special.

2. You are <u>free</u>.

   (Briefly explain to your guys the idea that many people think for someone to be a good Christian, he needs to do certain things. Have them try to fill in the blank of the lie, 2A. There's no real answer, just any of the unwritten rules Christians think we might need to follow.)

A. Lie: If you want to be a good Christian, then you need to _____.

B. "The former regulation is set aside because it was weak and useless (for the law made nothing perfect), and a better hope is introduced, by which we draw near to God." (Hebrews 7:18-19)

(The idea of laws making us better and better and eventually perfect was weak and useless. It's impossible. Instead trying to follow every law makes us feel worse and worse. This better hope brings us closer to God.)

C. "It is for freedom that Christ has set us free. Stand firm, then, and do not let yourselves be burdened again by a yoke of slavery." (Galatians 5:1)

(That yoke of slavery is the idea of trying to do things to get God to love us more. Here are the problems with trying to follow these rules and laws as if they are what save us:

▷ *It puts us in control.*

▷ *It leads to either pride or guilt.*

▷ *It creates lots of pressure.*

▷ *It makes us fear God.*

▷ *It makes us want to break out, to rebel.*

▷ *It gives no joy.*

In contrast to laws, grace draws you toward Jesus. It makes you want to love him more.

When you know you don't have to do anything to get God to like you more, it makes you want to get to know him more and be like him. There's nothing you have to do; you're free.

Lastly, share this great quote from Dallas Willard and talk about what it means.)

"What would you do if you knew that there was nothing to do?"

—Dallas Willard

OUTLINE

IDENTITY, PART TWO: YOU ARE A NEW CREATION, HOLY AND FREE

1. You have been made h_____.

   A. "Once you were alienated from God and were enemies in your minds because of your evil behavior. But now he has reconciled you by Christ's physical body through death to present you holy in his sight, without blemish and free from accusation." (Colossians 1:21-22)

   B. "It is because of him that you are in Christ Jesus, who has become for us wisdom from God—that is, our righteousness, holiness and redemption." (1 Corinthians 1:30)

   C. You are one in whom C_____ dwells. You are s_____ and special.

2. You are f_____.

   A. Lie: If you want to be a good Christian, then you need to _____.

   B. "The former regulation is set aside because it was weak and useless (for the law made nothing perfect), and a better hope is introduced, by which we draw near to God." (Hebrews 7:18-19)

   C. "It is for freedom that Christ has set us free. Stand firm, then, and do not let yourselves be burdened again by a yoke of slavery." (Galatians 5:1)

"What would you do if you knew that there was nothing to do?" —Dallas Willard

MANLY MAN INTERVIEW

This week's **Soul Work** has two parts.

Part One

Get your dad to help you find a Bible verse or verses related to being responsible, taking care of things, fulfilling needs or obligations, or taking care of others. (If your dad isn't available, ask any older Christian guy you respect.)

The Bible has tons of stories about this, so I don't want to hear any, "I couldn't find anything...uh, between commercials and video games...I was so busy...."

1. What verse or verses did you come up with? _____

2. What's the story about or what does the verse mean?

Part Two

Call one of the older guys from your church on the phone and ask him the following questions. (Make sure to write down his responses).

3. What kinds of things were you responsible for as a boy?

4. How are responsibilities for boys different now than when you were a kid?

5. When it comes to responsibility, when does a boy become a man?

6. What do you feel is a man's single most important responsibility?

7. How can I begin to be more responsible?

8. Who was a great model of being responsible for you while you were growing up?

CHAPTER SIX

FINISHING THE TASK: MEN ARE RESPONSIBLE

THE BIG IDEA

A boy becomes a man when he's responsible.

Main Text

> When I was a child, I talked like a child, I thought like a child, I reasoned like a child. When I became a man, I put the ways of childhood behind me. (1 Corinthians 13:11)

What's the Point?

We spent the first three sessions dealing with students' minds, their heads, asking, "What's a man supposed to think?" and tearing down the myths about being a real man. The last two sessions we've focused on our guys' hearts, asking, "What's a man supposed to feel?" and unlocking a God-centered identity. Now we'll begin the practical portion of the book by focusing on the guys' hands, asking, "What's a man supposed to do?" And we'll introduce the idea that a boy becomes a man NOT when he first hits puberty, has sex, or accomplishes some crazy "manly" feat. Instead he becomes a man when he becomes responsible for himself.

RECAP SOUL WORK

Last week your guys were supposed to get their dads (or other males in their lives) to help them find Bible verses on being responsible and interview grandfather-type gentlemen from church. Go through their interviews and talk about what these men said about responsibilities and the differences between when they were boys and how guys are today.

If your guys didn't come through, give them each 40 lashes minus one and talk about how this idea of responsibility relates to you personally and to grandfathers. (Just kidding about the lashes!) After you discuss their interviews, move on to the **Opening Activity.**

OPENING ACTIVITY
Option One: Manliness Test

Ask your guys, **What, in your mind, makes a guy manly?** If your guys are being too spiritual, ask them, **What do most guys consider manly?** or, **When does our culture say a boy becomes a man?** *(Possible answers: the onset of puberty, losing your virginity, getting a job and living on your own, doing some crazy stunt; your first beer, first job, first kiss; voting; turning 21, etc.)*

After they've given their answers, tell them you're going to have them participate in a manliness test to see how manly they really are. You can have them do one or both of the tests to demonstrate manliness.

▷ Test #1: Eating Contest

Treat this contest like a hot dog eating contest or any one of the "extreme eating" competitions. You can see how fast your guys will eat ice cream or any other food they can't choke on.

▷ Test #2: "Mensa" Contest

Maybe you also want to test the guys' thinking abilities. You can have some giant math problem to see who can solve it fastest. Here's an example:

$1{,}265 \times 45 + 698 - 77 = 57{,}546$

After all your winners have been declared, transition to the **Big Picture** by saying something like, **Today we're going to talk about when a boy really becomes a man. And we're going to take a look at three manly guys in the Bible.**

Pray for your guys and jump in.

Prizes for your manly game and puzzle winners; ice cream or other "non-choking" food (if you choose to do the eating contest); a big piece of butcher paper or a posterboard, chalkboard, or whiteboard; someone's dad lined up to share; Tootsie Roll banks, piggy banks, or precut wood and nails, hammer, etc., to make your own banks; gold foil-covered chocolate coins; some cash

Option Two: Becoming a Man Story

Ask your guys, **What, in your mind, makes a guy manly?** If your guys are being too spiritual, ask them, W**hat do most guys consider manly?** or, **When does our culture say a boy become a man?** (The onset of puberty, losing your virginity, getting a job and living on your own, doing some crazy stunt; your first beer, first job, first kiss; voting; turning 21, etc.)

After they've given their answers, share with them from your life about how you grew up and what you thought it meant to become a man. What did you learn from your dad? What did it mean to you to be a man? What did you have to do to become one?

Bonus points: If you have any funny stories about puberty—for example, about the wispy moustache you had as a freshman, etc.—toss them in there. Your guys will laugh, and your story will give them great insight and hope.

Transition to the **Big Picture** by saying something like, **Today we're going to talk about when a boy really becomes a man. And we're going to take a look at three manly guys in the Bible.**

Pray for your guys and jump in.

Option Three: Rites of Passage

Unfortunately, in America we don't have a clear rite of passage for guys. Our culture doesn't make it clear when a boy becomes a man. However, a few cultures do have these ceremonies or had them at one point.

Talk about some of the rites of passages boys in some traditions have to go through. If you're familiar with other ones not mentioned here, talk about those. I've given you just a little information on three rites of passage to share.

1. *Jewish boys: Bar Mitzvah*

   When Jewish guys turn 13, they have these huge parties called bar mitzvahs. The 13-year-old boy reads from the Torah, and the Jewish community celebrates because the boy is now considered a man and can begin to take on the responsibilities of a grown-up man.

2. *Amish boys: Rumspringa*

In the Amish community teenagers are allowed to experience what life's like outside of the Amish community before they commit to being full members. This time is called Rumspringa. After the allotted amount of time of sampling the real world, the teenagers are given the opportunity to come back and be devout Amish or leave the community.

3. *Ancient Japanese boys: Genpuku*

Genpuku was a historical Japanese coming-of-age ceremony. To mark the entry into adult life of boys between the ages of 12 and 16, they were taken to shrines and presented with their first adult clothes. Their boys' hairstyles were changed to the adult men's style, and they were also given new adult names.

Ask your guys, **What are some, if there are any, modern-day rites of passages for guys?** *(The onset of puberty, losing your virginity, getting a job and living on your own, doing some crazy stunt; your first beer, first job, first kiss; voting; turning 21, etc.)*

Transition to the **Big Picture** by saying something like, **Today we're going to talk about when a boy really becomes a man. And we're going to take a look at three manly guys in the Bible.**

Pray for your guys and jump in.

THE BIG PICTURE

The **Big Picture** focuses on three Scriptures about three important guys: the Apostle Paul, King David, and the REAL man of all men, Jesus. You'll discuss what Paul means in 1 Corinthians 13:11 when he says he put childish ways behind him. We'll also take a look at David and how he took responsibility for a nation of cowards unwilling to fight Goliath. Finally, we'll hear from Jesus and his teaching on talents.

So grab your **Outline** (Leader Guide) and get going. After you're done, proceed to the **Breakdown**.

BREAKDOWN

Option One: Ways to Take More Responsibility

Now that you've challenged your guys to try to be more responsible, we need to get practical and give them some real help. They've already seen a few ways through the study—now let's take it even further.

Brainstorm with your guys and think of ways they can be responsible now. Create as long a list as you can. Here are some examples: Cleaning your room before you're asked, doing chores in the morning, doing homework right after school, limiting television, helping around the house, etc.

Once your group has compiled the largest list known to mankind, transition to the **Closing Activity** by saying, **As you do more and more of these things, your family will see you becoming more and more of a man. And then you'll receive the respect and benefits that trust and responsibility bring.**

Option Two: Dad Guest Speaker

Bring in a dad and have him talk about what it means to take responsibility and give the guys tips on how to be responsible now and ways they can grow in responsibility. You can bring in your own dad or even one of the guys' dads. Just make sure you find a dad you really respect and have him share from his life.

After the dad's time of sharing is done, ask the guys if they have any questions. Or you can ask some follow-up questions to try to make your speaker's words as practical as possible for your guys.

Thank your guest for sharing and say something like, **As you act more responsibly, your family will see you becoming more and more of a man. And then you'll receive the respect and benefits that trust and responsibility bring.**

Option Three: Manliness Acrostic

Now that your guys have had their eyes opened to the doorway of manhood, I'm sure they're begging you, saying, "Oh, great small group leader, tell me how I can become more responsible." Or not. Nevertheless, the next step is to give your guys some ideas on how they can begin this trek of manhood by being more responsible. Help them process this by handing out the **Are You M.A.N.L.Y.?** sheet.

You can either work through the acrostic as a team and think of ways to be more responsible together or have the kids work independently to fill out their sheets. Or if you're pressed for time and just need to give the guys some practical ideas, teach through my sample and have the dudes fill in the blanks.

My sample acrostic—

Make your bed in the morning.

Always do your homework right after school.

Notify your parents if you're going to get home late.

Leave your room clean and organized.

Instead of having your mom do it, start doing your own laundry.

Next time you get mad, talk calmly and listen intently.

Excite your parents by taking care of the pets.

Surprise your parents by saying yes instead of arguing.

Start to ask your parents for more opportunities for responsibility.

Have volunteers share what they came up with and then move to the **Closing Activity** by saying something like, **As you act more responsibly, your family will see you becoming more and more of a man. And then you'll receive the respect and benefits that trust and responsibility bring.**

CLOSING ACTIVITY
Option One: Trust Bank

Wayne Rice has a great illustration in his book *Read This Book or You're Grounded!* about trust.

His idea is to get every student to have a "trust bank" with his parents. Whenever your guy demonstrates honesty, integrity, and increased responsibility, he's depositing trust into his account. And every time he shows dishonesty, lies, or is irresponsible, it's like withdrawing trust from his account. When a guy's trust account is full, he can have tons of freedom. When his trust account is empty, he has no freedom.

> **MONEY TALK**
>
> Don't assume your guys understand how bank accounts work. You may need to go over deposits and withdrawals and the basics of banking to help them understand the trust bank illustration.

Share this illustration with your guys and make sure they get it. Go over the examples you came up with in the last section about responsibility and talk about how they relate to the trust bank idea.

After you talk about the trust bank, either have your guys build their own minibanks or give each guy a bank he can keep as a reminder of what you talked about. See the "Bank Ideas" sidebar for options on what you can do for banks.

Hand out the **Soul Work** for this week. Finally, close your time together by praying and asking God to help your guys begin putting trust into their accounts starting tonight.

Option Two: Chocolate Coins

Go over the trust bank illustration from **Option One.** Then instead of a bank, give each guy a bag of chocolate coins as a reminder to make deposits into his responsibility bank all week long. Or at least every time he eats a coin.

Hand out the **Soul Work** for this week. Finally, close your time together by praying and asking God to help your guys begin putting trust into their accounts starting tonight.

Option Three: The $100 Challenge

Remind your guys about the parable of the talents (Matthew 25:14-30). Then do what Jesus did. Give these guys some talents (i.e., some cash, $10 each, $5, whatever). Tell them they have one week to be responsible for the cash and next week you want a report from them on what they did with it.

Suggest some options such as holding the cash and not spending it (which could be a real test for my guys), doing something for God with their cash or investing it.

Then next week talk about what they did with their "talents" and how they demonstrated being responsible.

Hand out the **Soul Work** for this week and close your time together by praying. Ask God to help your guys start taking responsibility and becoming young men of God.

FINISHING THE TASK: MEN ARE RESPONSIBLE

1. There's a difference between a <u>man</u> and a <u>boy</u>.

   "When I was a child, I talked like a child, I thought like a child, I reasoned like a child. When I became a man, I put the ways of childhood behind me." (1 Corinthians 13:11)

   (Ask your guys, **What do you think Paul meant by talking like a child, thinking and reasoning like a child?** Clearly, at some point, a boy no longer talks, thinks, or reasons like a kid. Then ask them, **What are some of the differences between a boy and a man?**)

2. One manly dude: <u>David</u>

   Saul replied, "You are not able to go out against this Philistine and fight him; you are little more than a boy, and he has been a warrior from his youth." But David said to Saul, "Your servant has been keeping his father's sheep. When a lion or a bear came and carried off a sheep from the flock, I went after it, struck it and rescued the sheep from its mouth. When it turned on me, I seized it by its hair, struck it and killed it. Your servant has killed both the lion and the bear; this uncircumcised Philistine will be like one of them, because he has defied the armies of the living God. The LORD who rescued me from the paw of the lion and the paw of the bear will rescue me from the hand of this Philistine." Saul said to David, "Go, and the LORD be with you." (1 Samuel 17:33-37)

   (Tell the story of 1 Samuel 17. Emphasize when Saul says, "You are little more than a boy" and how David responds. Two things here are key:

   A. *People generally don't believe in middle schoolers. Their thinking is, "You can't do that—you're only boys," the same thing David was told. And yet David did something crazy...brave...and heroic.*

   B. *David took responsibility. David responds with proof that he isn't afraid and tells how he's killed far fiercer things than this giant Goliath. When no one else will fight, David takes on the responsibility. He trusts in God and leaves childhood far behind.*)

3. The manliest dude: Jesus

"His master replied, 'Well done, good and faithful servant! You have been faithful with a few things; I will put you in charge of many things. Come and share your master's happiness!'" (Matthew 25:21)

(Tell the story of Matthew 25:14-30, where Jesus teaches the Parable of the Talents and how he rewards those who are responsible and punishes the slacker. Point out that being responsible isn't this huge, overwhelming idea of growing up quick and not having fun anymore.

Jesus values responsibility. You don't have to take responsibility for giant, enormous things because...)

4. Being faithful with a few things is being responsible.

*(Talk about some things your guys can be faithful with and then move to the **Breakdown**.)*

FINISHING THE TASK: MEN ARE RESPONSIBLE

1. There's a difference between a m_____ and a b_____.

   "When I was a child, I talked like a child, I thought like a child, I reasoned like a child. When I became a man, I put the ways of childhood behind me." (1 Corinthians 13:11)

2. One manly dude: D_____

   Saul replied, "You are not able to go out against this Philistine and fight him; you are little more than a boy, and he has been a warrior from his youth." But David said to Saul, "Your servant has been keeping his father's sheep. When a lion or a bear came and carried off a sheep from the flock, I went after it, struck it and rescued the sheep from its mouth. When it turned on me, I seized it by its hair, struck it and killed it. Your servant has killed both the lion and the bear; this uncircumcised Philistine will be like one of them, because he has defied the armies of the living God. The LORD who rescued me from the paw of the lion and the paw of the bear will rescue me from the hand of this Philistine." Saul said to David, "Go, and the LORD be with you." (1 Samuel 17:33-37)

3. The manliest dude: J_____.

   "His master replied, 'Well done, good and faithful servant! You have been faithful with a few things; I will put you in charge of many things. Come and share your master's happiness!'" (Matthew 25:21)

4. Being faithful with a few things is being _____.

Use your mad skills to come up with some ideas on ways you can be more responsible now.

M _____

A _____

N _____

L _____

I _____

N _____

E _____

S _____

S _____

SOUL WORK

PROJECT ONE

Read the book of Jude. Really. It's in your Bible. It's actually the shortest book of the Bible. It'll take you five minutes to read. And that way you can say you've actually read one of the books of the Bible. Read Jude and then answer this question:

What is God saying through this book?

PROJECT TWO

Find a clock or a stopwatch and set it for five minutes. Sit in a chair, close your eyes, and be silent for five minutes. You may have to sit in your closet, your room, or your bathroom to get away from the family. While you're silent, inside your mind ask God this question: "What do you want to say to me, God?" Just say it over and over and over again and listen for a response. After your five minutes are up, answer this question:

What did God say to you in the silence?

PROJECT THREE

Think of some way to do something loving for your family. Maybe it's cleaning up something, helping out with some other chore, or writing a note of encouragement to someone in your family. Whatever you choose to do, do it and answer the following questions:

What did you do?

What's God trying to teach you through what you did?

PROJECT FOUR

Call or e-mail a minister at your church. Ask him or her this question and write down the response.

What is the number-one way you connect to and hear from God?

CHAPTER SEVEN

CROSS TRAINING: MEN TRAIN SPIRITUALLY FOR THE RACE THAT MATTERS

THE BIG IDEA

Real men have a relationship with God.

Main Text

> ...train yourself to be godly. For physical training is of some value, but godliness has value for all things, holding promise for both the present life and the life to come. (1 Timothy 4:7-8)

What's the Point?

From early on guys need to learn and practice spiritual disciplines to help them continue to experience the love and grace of God. We'll give them a crash course with simple beginnings and realistic progressions of disciplines they can begin practicing now.

RECAP SOUL WORK

Last week your guys had four projects. Whew! Go over your guys' experiences and talk about what they felt, thought, and did. For the few guys who did one or more of the projects, give it up for them and talk them up. Let them know how proud you are of them. Not only will it make them feel great and give them positive encouragement, but it'll also provide positive peer pressure for the other guys who forgot about doing it. And it'll give you a great lead-in to what we're talking about this session.

After you have your guys glowing, jump into the **Opening Activity.**

OPENING ACTIVITY

Option One: Getting to Know You

If you have some funny memories of middle school life that apply, give yourself 1,000 points for every girl who caught your eye—if you can name them to your guys.

All middle schoolers have some kind of ritual that goes along with dating or when a guy and a girl like each other. Some kind of "official" dating thing happens to move a relationship from friends to boyfriend-girlfriend. When I was in middle school, the phrase was "Will you go around with me?" which later morphed to "Will you go out with me?"

Tell your guys today you'll be talking about relationships, and if you can, recall this ridiculous dance of love to your guys. Then ask them some of the following questions:

> **So what's the official way a guy and a girl start a boyfriend-girlfriend relationship?**

> **How do guys and girls get to know each other?**

> **What are some of the steps guys and gals go through to get to know each other? What happens?**

> **How does that stuff relate to getting to know God?**

> **How does someone begin an official relationship with God?**

> **How does someone get to know God?**

YOU'LL NEED

A pair of old running shoes, shorts, sweatbands, etc.; one of your favorite sports movies; butcher paper, something to stick it to the wall with (or a chalkboard or whiteboard), and markers; some kind of video game or game based on skill (I had one youth volunteer who had students captivated as he used juggling to make his point; see the "Game Time" sidebar for a more thorough explanation); Burger King crowns

After your discussion of the dating rituals of modern-day young adolescents is finished, transition into the teaching part of this session by saying, **Getting to know God and having a relationship with God take work—just as in any regular relationship. Knowing and relating to God take practice; some might even say training.**

Share with them this verse from 1 Timothy: **"...train yourself to be godly. For physical training is of some value, but godliness has value for all things, holding promise for both the present life and the life to come" (1 Timothy 4:7-8).**

Then say, **Today I'm going to share with you three of the best training tips you can use to build a relationship with God.**

Have one of your guys pray for the group as you begin.

Rocky IV
Ah...Rocky versus Ivan Drago, or the U.S. versus Russia. If this training montage doesn't get you pumped for action, you clearly are not a child of the '80s. Play chapter 11: Hearts on Fire (start clip at 00:59:52, rocking guitar solo; stop at 01:04:05, Rocky yells, "AAHHH!").

Chariots of Fire
This short clip features Eric Liddell's coach training different runners for the upcoming Olympics. Play chapter 19: Training Montage (start clip at 00:54:17, guys running; stop at 00:56:13, surprise...another guy running).

Vision Quest
Complete with an awesome '80s soundtrack, this clip features wrestler Louden Swain (played by Matthew Modine) getting psyched about his upcoming match against the lumber-toting Brian Shute. Play chapter 28: Lunatic Fringe Workout (start clip at 01:33:34, Swain in a dark wrestling room; stop at 01:35:20, Swain fixing his singlet shoulder strap).

Option Two: Cross Training

Abstract Alert: This idea of relating the Christian life to a race is very abstract, and while some of your guys might totally get this, especially if they're involved in sports, some of your guys are going to have a hard time making the connection. Be sensitive to this and help them along if you think this option is appropriate.

We want to get our guys thinking about what it means to train their bodies for something. Grab your running gear and talk about working out and training for a marathon.

Then say, **You wouldn't go out there and just run a 10K in a business suit. No, you'd grab the right gear, get the right clothes—especially the right shoes—and you'd stretch and run shorter distances ahead of time to build up your endurance.**

If you have any funny stories about pulling muscles or training for a big football game (or baseball or whatever your sport), tell those and get into the idea about training hard so you could win. Make the point with this illustration that this is what it's like to train to live as a Christian man. Talk about how life is a marathon, not a sprint. And if you're going to make it to the finish line, if you're going to win, you'll need to have the right gear and the right training.

Share with them this verse from 1 Timothy: **"...train yourself to be godly. For physical training is of some value, but godliness has value for all things, holding promise for both the present life and the life to come" (1 Timothy 4:7-8).**

Then say, **Today I'm going to share with you three of the best training tips to help you finish this race.**

Pick someone from your group to pray for your time together.

Option Three: Training Clips

Abstract Alert: This idea, like **Option Two**, can be a bit tricky. Try your best to show very clearly the connection between training for a sport and training to live as a Christian man. Some of your guys might have trouble connecting the dots.

Grab one of your favorite sports movies and cue it up to a scene with someone training for an event. If you're short on time or need some ideas, check the "Training Clips" sidebar for three choices.

Ask your guys if they've ever had to train for an event or competition of some kind. Next tell them you found an old clip of yourself working out for a competition and thought they'd like to see what you used to look like as a teen. Then watch the sports movie clip.

Now that you're totally pumped and your guys are laughing hard, go through these questions:

> ▷ **What was the guy doing in the movie?** *(Possible—and desired— answer: Training!)*

> ▷ **What kinds of things was he doing to train?**

> ▷ **Why and how were those activities helping him?**

Then say something like, **In a lot of ways living as a Christian man is like training for a race. The goal is to finish the race, and it's not a sprint but a marathon. You don't want to end up on the disabled list or on the side of the road. You want to finish strong.**

Share with them this verse from 1 Timothy: **"...train yourself to be godly. For physical training is of some value, but godliness has value for all things, holding promise for both the present life and the life to come" (1 Timothy 4:7-8).**

Continue with, **And godly living takes training of a different kind. Instead of training to be athletes, we want to train to be men of God, real men. Today I'm going to share with you three training techniques you can use now to help you finish the race.**

Have one guy from your group pray for your time together as you learn about what it means to finish this race.

THE BIG PICTURE

You're going to go over three spiritual practices: Contemplative prayer, Bible reading, and serving. This isn't meant to explain spiritual practices thoroughly for students. Instead it's more of a realistic kick start. You'll have the guys actually choose one of the three disciplines to go through in the next section.

Be real. Share your failures at living as a Christian man, which are likely easier to talk about than your successes.

Most of us feel so much shame, we don't read our entire Bible through every 90 days; our morning prayers begin at the stoplight on the way to work and end with the chorus on the radio; and Jesus doesn't appear at our bedside every day just to shoot the breeze.

Talk with your guys about your struggle to study God's Word and listen to the Holy Spirit. Do also share with them times when you've heard God's voice or found something unexpectedly encouraging in the Bible.

Let your kids know you're a real person, not an unapproach-able "Super Christian" (unless you are a Super Christian—then you can pray for the rest of us).

Introduce the group to these spiritual disciplines (otherwise known as training tips) and the Scriptures that encourage our efforts to grow in our faith. At the bottom of the **Outline** is a commitment form for the training tip to do next week. Tell the guys you're going to fill out the form together at the end of today's time.

Here is a quick summary of the three training tips.

1. *Contemplative Prayer:* **Most of our prayers are either shopping lists or desperate cries for help. However, for some of the earliest Christians, prayer was more about listening than about talking. When we quiet ourselves and listen attentively for God, we often hear God speak to our souls.**

   Go on, **An easy way to begin is by starting with three to five minutes. You pick one of the following things to focus on:**

   A. **A picture in your mind that reminds you of God, maybe a painting you've seen or a statue. You could picture yourself spending time with God, walking, talking, etc. Think and focus on the picture silently and listen.**

   B. **"The Jesus Prayer" is a famous way Christians before you have radically experienced God. Here's a form of this prayer you can say to God over and over and over again: "Lord Jesus Christ, son of God, have mercy on me, a sinner."**

   C. **Ask God a question over and over again and listen for his answer. Your question could be something simple, such as, "God, what do you want me to do?"**

2. *Bible Reading.* **Reading God's Word has always seemed like a "quantity equals quality" or "more means better" type deal to me. And yet I've found just the opposite is true.**

   Instead of focusing on how many chapters we can read each day, focus on a few verses to read at each sitting. Maybe one of Jesus' parables (or stories). Or maybe a psalm. Maybe just two or three verses from a letter from Paul. Whichever you choose, make it short and fairly simple. Then read the verse or verses.

   After you've read them, read them again. And again. Think about what this text means and how it applies to your life.

Is God trying to tell you something? Is there something you need to do because of this verse? What does it mean to you?

If it makes sense, mentally put yourself in the story. How would you feel if you were there? What would you think? How would you respond to the situation?

Some easy passages to begin with are Psalm 1, Psalm 23, John 8:1-11, and Philippians 2:5-11.

3. *Serving others.* One of the most practical ways of experiencing God and developing a relationship with God is through serving other people. You have numerous ways you could do this—opening a door for people, doing others' chores for them, clearing dishes off the table, vacuuming the living room, carrying groceries, playing with a child, cooking dinner, mowing the lawn, washing the car, doing the laundry, renting a movie someone else wants to see even when you've seen it and hate it, etc.

The idea is, instead of being self-focused, you choose to help other people. Jesus said he came not to be served, but to serve (Matthew 20:28). Mother Teresa spent her life ministering to the poorest of the poor because she was not serving people, but God.

When you purposefully look for ways to serve others and follow through, you experience God in new and exciting ways. The hardest part may be making your list of things to do.

There's so much more to say. For now share from your experience on all three of these training tips. Share how you've gotten closer to God through listening to him. Talk about verses that've shaped your life. Tell the guys about times you felt you were serving God as you bought a lunch for a homeless guy hanging outside a gas station, etc.

When you finish, move to the **Breakdown** by saying, **Now you have some training tips, so it's time to practice.**

BREAKDOWN

Have the group agree on one of the three disciplines to practice during your time together since you probably won't have time for them to try all three.

Option One: Listening to God through Contemplative Prayer

If your guys pick to listen, have them each pick something to focus on or a question to ask. Say a simple prayer asking God to help everyone listen and give them five minutes.

When the time's up, ask some of the following questions:

▷ **What did God say to you? Did any of you feel as if God spoke to you?**

▷ **What did you use to focus on—a picture? A word? A question? The Jesus Prayer?**

▷ **How did you feel—bored? Relaxed? Or something else?**

▷ **Did five minutes seem fast or slow?**

▷ **Did you find yourself easily distracted, filled with ideas of all kinds of things besides God?**

▷ **Did you feel as though God was with you or not?**

▷ **What time could you do this every day?**

▷ **How would you feel about journaling about your times doing this?**

After your guys have finished, jump into the **Closing Activity** by saying something like, **Keep practicing the art of listening. It's like tuning a radio or TV antenna. Soon you'll be able to pick up the perfect frequency, and you'll be experiencing a new kind of life.**

Option Two: Bible Reading

Get out the Bibles if they picked this option. Use the suggested passages from the **Outline** and have the young men decide whether they all want to focus on the same text or have each guy pick an individual Scripture passage to go through. Either way has positive aspects. You'll either hear how the same text affects each guy a bit differently, how different texts ministered separately, or...how hard it was to stay awake.

Once the group has made the decision on which passage(s) to read, watch the clock for five minutes. If they chose separate passages, have each guy share what he read and what it means to him. If they chose the same passage, go around and have each guy talk about what stood out in the text to him. Then use these questions for further discussion.

▷ **How was this way of reading the Bible different than what you've done before?**

▷ **Was it hard to concentrate on the text without your mind wandering? Why or why not?**

▷ **How did you feel as you read the text?**

▷ **How does reading the Bible like this help?**

After your guys have finished, jump into the **Closing Activity** by saying something like, **I hope this will really help you experience your Bible in a new, exciting, and fun way. Keep working at it. Savor your reading. Enjoy it.**

Option Three: Serving Others

If your guys decided to try serving others as an option, spend this time thinking of the most practical ways they can serve others around them. Slap a paper on the wall (or use chalkboard or whiteboard) and have one of your guys be the scribe for the list. Have your students dream as big or as little or as goofy or as serious as they want. Get them thinking of as many ways they can serve others as possible.

After the list is complete and the ideas have finally focused, ask them some of these questions:

▷ **Look at the list. How many of those things could you do nearly every day?**

▷ **Which of the ideas would positively impact the most people?**

▷ **Which idea is your favorite?**

▷ **Which idea, if you did it, would make your family or friends take notice?**

▷ **What keeps people from doing the things on the list?**

• High-Dollar Version: You'll need an Xbox 360, a Wii, or a PS3; a TV; and a game.

• Low-Cost Version: One of those $10 video game and joystick combos you just plug into your TV so you can play all those sweet Atari games like Pac-Man.

• No-Cost Version: Invite a student to bring his video game system and a game to the church.

One of my volunteers didn't have any video games, but he did have an obscure skill: Juggling. The students were absolutely captivated as he talked about how he practiced juggling over and over again as a kid and became very good at it.

Then he related that to practicing spiritual disciplines. No video games? No worries.

▷ **Which one of those ideas will you do?**

Share some way you've served someone before, how you felt, and whether you felt God was very pleased with you.

After you finish, jump into the **Closing Activity** by saying something like, **Serving people by demonstrating God's love in a practical way usually ends up encouraging and strengthening someone...you. I pray you'll experience incredible growth as you serve others.**

CLOSING ACTIVITY
Option One: Practice Makes Perfect

Abstract Alert: Again, this idea is very abstract, but your guys can get it.

Close out today's session by playing some kind of game of skill with your guys. If you can secure a video game, this will really hit home with them. Introduce the idea by saying something like, **As we end tonight, I thought we'd play a quick game.** Then play the game.

You won't have a whole lot of time left, so just play for five minutes and then stop the game to ask some of the following questions. (I've written these as if you were playing video games. If you didn't do video games, just adapt the questions.)

▷ **How old were you guys when you started playing video games?**

▷ **What was it like when you started? Were you any good?**

▷ **Do you remember the first time you beat a game? What was that like? Did it take a long time? How did you feel afterward?**

▷ **Are you better at video games now than you were when you began playing? Why?**

▷ **How is playing video games like doing our training tips?**

Help them connect the dots about how when they started playing video games, they were clumsy and could hardly play without losing quickly. Then with practice they grew more and more skilled and eventually knew the buttons without looking and could finish the games.

If you can relate to them by recalling a time playing Super Mario Bros. or Joust on the Atari, use that story. Get into it! And relate it back to practicing the spiritual training tips.

You might say something like, **When we first start reading our Bibles, listening to God, or serving other people, it can seem boring, clumsy, and hard to do well. But eventually, when you do it enough, when you practice, you get really good.**

Continue, **Even while you're clumsy, you're building and developing a relationship with God. You're training for godliness, training to reign in heaven with God. And developing a friendship with God you'll always have.**

Close out your time together by having them finish the bottom of their **Outlines**. Have each guy pick a training tip to do during the week, at what time, for how long, etc. Hand out the **Soul Work** for this week, pray, and you're done.

Option Two: Training for Reigning

Tip: You may or may not have already utilized the ol' Burger King crowns when we talked about being children of the King. Even if you did, you still may be able to pull this off, so make sure you have enough crowns for all your guys.

After you give a crown to each guy and have him wearing it, looking really kingly, ask the group, **What types of things would a young prince do to get ready to become king one day?** *(He'd probably take lots of fighting classes, be well-versed in culture, and learn from the wisest people available. More than anything he'd probably talk to the king as much as possible.)*

Close your time together by challenging the guys to take these training tips seriously. And remind them one day they'll be in heaven, reigning as some of the princes of heaven. So until they're in heaven, they're here, training for reigning.

Say something like, **These training tips will help get you ready to experience life with God. By listening to God and reading God's Word, you get connected one-on-one with the Creator of the universe. When you serve someone, you fight against your selfish desires and help someone else. This really is training for reigning.**

Close out your time together by having them finish the bottom of their **Outline**. Have each guy pick a training tip to do during the week, at what time, for how long, etc. Hand out the **Soul Work** for this week, pray, and you're done.

Option Three: Pick a Time and a Realistic Goal

I get it. You're pressed for time. You had to work late and forgot it was your week to lead. No problem.

Worst-case scenario: Have your guys finish the bottom of their **Outline**. Have each student pick one of the training tips to practice this week and write down specifically when, where, how long, and what he plans to do.

Once all your guys are locked in, pray, hand out this week's **Soul Work**, and you're done!

CROSS TRAINING: MEN TRAIN SPIRITUALLY FOR THE RACE THAT MATTERS

"However, I consider my life worth nothing to me; my only aim is to finish the race and complete the task the Lord Jesus has given me—the task of testifying to the good news of God's grace." (Acts 20:24)

*(Paul says the only thing that matters is finishing the race. Ask the guys, **What race is Paul talking about?** Finishing the task of telling people about God's love and grace is the answer. How can the guys do that? By practicing the three following training tips.)*

Three training tips to get you ready for the race

1. Listening

   "Very early in the morning, while it was still dark, Jesus got up, left the house and went off to a solitary place, where he prayed." (Mark 1:35)

   (We didn't get to see what Jesus' training tips were, but this verse gives us insight into what one may've been.)

   An easy way to begin is by starting with three to five minutes. Pick one of the following things to focus on:

   ▷ a picture in your mind that reminds you of God

   ▷ a word that reminds you of God

   ▷ the "Jesus Prayer": "Lord Jesus Christ, Son of God, have mercy on me, a sinner."

   ▷ a question to ask God

2. Bible reading

   Instead of focusing on how many chapters you can read each day, focus on a few verses at each sitting. Maybe it's one of Jesus' parables. Or maybe a psalm. Maybe just two or three verses from a letter from Paul.

   Try one of these: Psalm 1, Psalm 23, John 8:1-11, or Philippians 2:5-11.

3. Serving others

    "The Son of Man did not come to be served, but to serve." (Matthew 20:28)

    One of the most practical ways of experiencing God and developing a relationship with him is through serving other people. Rather than being self-focused, you choose to help other people instead of doing your own thing.

4. Which training tip will you practice this week?

    Training tip: _____

    How many times? _____

    At what time? _____

    For how long? _____

CROSS TRAINING: MEN TRAIN SPIRITUALLY FOR THE RACE THAT MATTERS

"However, I consider my life worth nothing to me; my only aim is to finish the race and complete the task the Lord Jesus has given me—the task of testifying to the good news of God's grace." (Acts 20:24)

Three training tips to get you ready for the race

1. L_____

   "Very early in the morning, while it was still dark, Jesus got up, left the house and went off to a solitary place, where he prayed." (Mark 1:35)

   An easy way to begin is by starting with three to five minutes. Pick one of the following things to focus on:

   ▷ a picture in your mind that reminds you of God

   ▷ a word that reminds you of God

   ▷ the "Jesus Prayer": "Lord Jesus Christ, Son of God, have mercy on me, a sinner."

   ▷ a question to ask God

2. B_____ r_____

   Instead of focusing on how many chapters you can read each day, focus on a few verses at each sitting. Maybe it's one of Jesus' parables. Or maybe a psalm. Maybe just two or three verses from a letter from Paul.

   Try one of these: Psalm 1, Psalm 23, John 8:1-11, or Philippians 2:5-11.

3. S_____ o_____

   "The Son of Man did not come to be served, but to serve." (Matthew 20:28)

   One of the most practical ways of experiencing God and developing a relationship with him is through serving other people. Rather than being self-focused, you choose to help other people instead of doing your own thing.

4. Which training tip will you practice this week?

    Training tip: _____

    How many times? _____

    At what time? _____

    For how long? _____

SOUL WORK

When it comes to middle school guys doing great things for God, most people respond just as King Saul did in 1 Samuel 17:33. David, the shepherd boy, was ready to fight the giant Goliath. When he said he was ready, Saul said, "You are little more than a boy."

David was ready to do something incredible with his life. Are you? One guy already is, and I want you to know more about him. His name is Zach Hunter, and he's spending his life fighting slavery. He's been on TV, has spoken around the world to hundreds of thousands of people, and has even written his own book called *Be the Change*.

How old is Zach? What do you think? Maybe you guessed it...he's 15. Do you know when he started? Hmmm? He started a ministry collecting change to help end slavery (called "Loose Change to Loosen Chains" or LC2LC) when he was in seventh grade.

On Zach's LC2LC MySpace page you'll find this quotation: "I founded Loose Change to Loosen Chains because I felt a need to do something to bring freedom to the victims I was learning about. LC2LC is a group of students and emerging leaders who want to see the trade in human beings stopped. Modern-day slavery may be people working in brick kilns, rice mills, fishing villages, or brothels. Together we can make a difference. Let's abolish slavery!"

Find out more about Zach by going to the following Web sites this week:

www.theamazingchange.com/zach.html

www.myspace.com/amazingchange

www.myspace.com/lc2lc

Zach rocks. But enough about him. Let's talk about you.

Check out this verse from Ephesians 2:10: "For we are God's handiwork, created in Christ Jesus to do good works, which God prepared in advance for us to do."

According to this verse...

1. We are God's _____.

2. What does that mean?

3. We were created in Christ Jesus to do...what?

4. God prepared WHEN for us to do these things?

5. Another way of saying that would be _____.

You got your dad with you? If your dad is unavailable, grab another adult who knows you really well and finish up this page.

God has created you—YOU—to do good works. So let's talk about that. (By the way, you don't need to write down the answers to the next five questions; just talk about them with the adult you've chosen.)

▷ What has God stirred up in your heart?

▷ How does God want to use you to change the world?

▷ What are you passionate about?

▷ If you could change something to help people experience the love of God, what would you do?

▷ How can you make a difference in the lives of others?

Now for the real fun. Ask the adult you've chosen these questions and use the other side of this page to write down his answers.

▷ If God were to do something incredible through my life, what do you see that possibly being?

▷ What are some ways God can use me now to make a difference in the lives of other people?

Nice job. You CAN do it. You only have one life. Do something with it!

CHAPTER EIGHT

MEN AT WORK: LEADING IN MINISTRY

THE BIG IDEA

This is your last study of this book—time to drive home the point that real young men of God serve and help others.

Main Text

> "For we are God's handiwork, created in Christ Jesus to do good works, which God prepared in advance for us to do." (Ephesians 2:10)

What's the Point?

God has created each of us for ministry. The challenge will be for the guys to step up to the plate and begin actively serving in the church or a service organization or create ministries of their own designed to help others.

RECAP SOUL WORK

Last week we had the guys do two things: They learned about a 15-year-old kid named Zach Hunter who started a ministry called Loose Change 2 Loosen Chains. They were also to work with their dads, or dad-like figures, and talk about creating ministries of their very own.

They may or may not have figured out good ideas for ministry. That's okay because it'll have whetted their appetites for what we're talking about today. Ask the guys these questions about Zach.

> **What do you think of Zach?**

> **What surprised you about him?**

> **Why is what Zach's doing so significant?**

Then ask them how they did figuring out ministries of their very own. Go through what they came up with. (If their ministry was to burp during prayer time, remind them to practice that gift outside of small group time.)

Affirm and encourage whatever they came up with. Transition to your opener by saying something like, **Great job, guys! Today we're going to bring an end to this study course about becoming a man of God by talking about the final thing a real man does: Ministry.**

OPENING ACTIVITY

Option One: *Chariots of Fire*

Ask your guys, **What one thing can you do really well? Not necessarily an athletic thing—it can be ANYTHING: Making paper airplanes, shuffling cards, playing video games, jumping, picking your nose with your tongue, etc.**

Have each of your guys share what his one skill is and, if possible, demonstrate. Once you've gone through all the guys, introduce your clip with this brief setup: **Back in the early 1920s a young British runner named Eric Liddell was considered the fastest man in the world. Runners trained and trained to be faster than Eric so they could win the gold medal in the 1924 Olympics. Liddell had a crazy way of running with his head back and his mouth open. It was very unorthodox. But he had an incredible reason why he ran that way.**

Show chapter 34: 400 Meters; Divine Pleasure (start clip at 01:53:56, the racers line up; stop at 01:56:00, people clapping). Then ask these questions:

> **When Eric runs, he says he feels something. What is it?**

> **He says he feels God's pleasure. What does that mean?**

> **Do you ever do anything that makes you feel the same way?**

YOU'LL NEED

Chariots of Fire DVD; some kind of two-player game, such as cards, Connect 4, Battleship, basketball, sumo wrestling, or a two-player video game if you have video game access (or bust out the ol' 1980s system and play a rousing game of Pong); butcher paper and finger paints; a cheap football for the winning team for your *Win, Lose or Draw* game; water, basin, soap, and towel to dry feet; several inexpensive hand towels, one per guy; a guest to interview

YOU'LL NEED

Chariots of Fire DVD; some kind of two-player game, such as cards, Connect 4, Battleship, basketball, sumo wrestling, or a two-player video game if you have video game access (or bust out the ol' 1980s system and play a rousing game of Pong); butcher paper and finger paints; a cheap football for the winning team for your *Win, Lose or Draw* game; water, basin, soap, and towel to dry feet; several inexpensive hand towels, one per guy; a guest to interview

Then say something like, **As we'll see later, God has created you for good works. When you're doing what God has created you for, you feel just the way Eric does. You feel God's pleasure. Today I hope to help you begin to find out what God has created you for. When you do what God created you for, you'll feel God's pleasure.**

Have the fastest guy in your group pray for your time together and then head into the **Big Picture.**

Option Two: Feeling Left Out

Pick one of your guys to play your two-player game with you. Play your game and have everyone watch. Some of your guys might beg to play. Tell them no and say they might get a chance later, but for right now, it's just the two of you. But you're not actually going to let anyone else play because the point you're trying to drive home is the feeling of being left out.

After you've beaten your hapless opponent to a pulp, have a seat and ask some of these questions:

▷ **How did it feel to watch us play the game? Why?**

▷ **What do you like better, playing or watching...and why?** (*Also make sure to ask your opponent how it felt to play instead of sit.*)

▷ **How many of you guys have ever played on a team and had to sit on the bench or not get to play as much as you wanted? How did that feel?**

▷ **How does that relate to serving the church and being a Christian?**

Abstract Alert: The point you're trying to drive home is that it's more fun to do ministry than to watch ministry being done. And you feel important doing ministry; you feel great. Your guys may not catch on to this, so you might need to paint the picture for them.

If your guys were getting angry, frustrated, hacked, or really wanted to play, relate that to the point you're trying to make. That is to say, you should feel those same things if you aren't able to serve others in some way and make a difference.

Ask, **When it comes to God using someone to make a difference to show his love, would you rather be a player or sit on the bench? Why?**

Then say something like, **God has created you to do something amazing. When you're doing what God has created you for, it's fun. Today I hope to help you begin to find out what God has created you for so you can get off the bench and into the game.**

Have the fastest guy in your group pray for your time together and then head to the **Big Picture**.

Option Three: Vote with Your Feet

Explain to your guys you're going to read through pairs of options, and they each have to choose one or the other by standing up and moving to a certain designated wall or area in the room. For example: "Which color do you prefer? Red or green? If you like red, go to the wall on the left. If you like green, go to the wall on the right." They can't straddle the fence. They have to choose one option or the other.

Here's the list of options to have the guys vote on:

1. Coke or Pepsi

2. Roller coasters or bumper cars

3. Ice cream or cookies

4. Baseball or football

5. Pepperoni or sausage

6. Bubble gum or sunflower seeds

7. Car or truck

8. Texting or IMing

9. Movies or bowling

10. Hanging out with your buddies or doing your chores

Bonus: rock, paper, or scissors

Once you finish, have the guys take a seat and ask them some of these questions:

▷ **Of the 10 pairs of options, which one was your favorite to have to choose between?**

▷ **Which were hard to decide?**

> ▷ **When you think of all those things you like best—you know, driving a truck, eating ice cream, going on roller coasters—what are some of the feelings you have?**

> ▷ **Of all those things, which one of those could you do all day and not feel as if you're missing anything?**

After your questions transition to the **Big Picture** by saying something like, **Number 10 was a no-brainer. We'd all rather hang out with our bros than do chores. When it comes to serving God, most people think it's about as much fun as doing your chores. But that's not how God designed good works. In fact, today we're going to discover how when you're doing what God created you to do, you'll have one of the best feelings in the world.**

Have the fastest guy in your group pray for your time together, then head to the **Big Picture**.

THE BIG PICTURE
Win, Lose or Draw with Your Feet

Back in the '90s there was a game show called *Win, Lose or Draw*. Two teams would compete for points by drawing pictures. Each team would choose an artist, and the rest of the team would be guessers. The team that guessed the most pictures correctly won. Same idea here, except we're doing a shorter version.

Split the guys into two teams and go over the rules: **Each team must select an artist. The artist will be given five things to draw. The artist can't talk or move, except to draw. He must draw pictures, and his team must guess the objects. If a team can't guess what their artist draws, the other team can steal the item and score points by guessing correctly.**

Have each team pick an artist. Then tell the guys there's only one catch: The artists have to draw their pictures with their bare feet. They can either paint by footprint or try to "finger paint" with their toes. Whatever works.

Usually, the game has multiple rounds. For this session just have one round. Pick five things for each artist to draw and list them on two note cards. Here's an example (or pick your own):

Team 1

▷ Tree

▷ Apple

▷ Angel

▷ Mouse

▷ Pencil

Team 2

▷ Cat

▷ Book

▷ Milk

▷ Hair

▷ Gut

Give the artists the note cards. The team that guesses the most in two minutes wins. Congratulate the winning team and hand them their "football" (insert groan here).

Tell your guys to take seats. Then grab your soap, water, and basin and take them to the players with the messy feet. Wash their feet and share with them a quick overview of John 13.

Then say something to the effect of, **On the night Jesus was arrested, he took time to teach his disciples their most important lesson so far: Serve one another. We can do nothing greater than to spend our lives serving people just as Jesus did.**

Pass out this week's **Outline** and go through it. But make sure to NOT do the "Moving into Ministry" part until you move to the **Breakdown**. You'll actually complete the sheets during that time.

BREAKDOWN

For today's **Breakdown** you'll have your guys complete the "Moving into Ministry" portion of their **Outlines**. Go ahead and introduce the idea something like this: **Now that we've talked about the two different kinds of ministries, we're going to finish the rest of your Outlines,** the part titled "Moving into Ministry." Our goal is for each one of you to become a man of God. Part of being a man is doing ministry. Before you fill in your Outlines, let me go over what each level means, and then you'll decide the next step you're willing to take.

Hand out the separate **Moving into Ministry** sheet to help explain the levels of involvement. Briefly go through what each ministry commitment level means based on the sports terms given. Then give your guys a few minutes to finish the "Moving into Ministry" section on the back of their **Outline**. Have each of them share some of the ministries he's thinking about doing.

After everyone's done sharing, tell them how proud you are of them and move on to the **Closing Activity.**

CLOSING ACTIVITY
Option One: Hand-Towel Handout

Close out your time together by giving each one of your guys a hand towel as a reminder of what Jesus did for the disciples. Say, **Just as Jesus took a towel to wash his disciples' feet, I'm giving you a towel as a reminder of what a real man is: A servant.**

Encourage each guy to put this towel on his dresser or bed or somewhere he'll see it as a reminder that real men serve in ministry. Share with the group again the words of Jesus when he says, "I have set you an example that you should do as I have done for you" (John 13:15).

They don't have to wait till they're older to do ministry. They can do life-changing ministry NOW. It's up to them to get off the bench and get in the game.

Close your time by praying for each of your guys by name; pray each will have the courage to get off the bench and jump into ministry. After you end your time in prayer, you'll want to leave the room before all the towel snapping begins. After you yell at the guys, wish them a great week, invite them to continue studying in the next series *(Living as a Young Man of God)*, and pray for them.

Option Two: Guest Interview

Close out your time together by bringing in someone to interview. Invite a guy in your church who's involved in some sort of ministry and ask him some of the following questions:

▷ **How long have you been attending our church?**

▷ **What ministry or ministries are you involved in?**

▷ **How long have you been doing this?**

▷ **How did you get started?**

▷ **Why do you do it?**

▷ **What would you say to a bunch of guys who just finished being challenged to start serving in ministry now instead of waiting till they're older?**

Close your time together by inviting your guys again to jump into ministry. They can do real valuable ministry NOW as middle school students. Then invite them to continue studying in the next series (*Living as a Young Man of God*), and then pray for each of your guys by name; pray each will have the courage to get off the bench and jump into ministry.

Option Three: Ye Olde Starfish Story

Close your time together by telling your guys this old story about the kid and the starfish. This isn't a new story, and it's a bit cheesy but it communicates.

> **There was once a little boy walking along the beach, and all of a sudden he came upon thousands of starfish washed up on the beach. The tide was going out, and for some strange reason the starfish ended up stuck on the beach.**
>
> **They were all doomed because they couldn't survive being out of the water in the hot sun until the next high tide. The little boy realized this and frantically started picking up starfish and throwing them, one at a time, back into the water.**

A man who was walking along the beach saw the boy doing this and yelled at the boy, "Son, what in the world are you doing? Don't you know there are thousands of starfish on this beach? And don't you know this beach goes on for miles and miles? There's no way in the world you can save all those starfish!"

The little boy thought about that for a moment, then turned to the man, picked up a starfish, and said, "Yeah, I know. But I can save this one." And he heaved it as far as he could into the ocean.[4]

Challenge your guys to get off the bench and do something. Encourage them to see that real men do ministry, and when they're doing what God created them to do, they ARE making a difference, even if it doesn't look that way to other people. Then invite them to continue studying in the next series *(Living as a Young Man of God)*, and close your time by praying for each of your guys by name; pray each will have the courage to get off the bench and jump into ministry.

[4] Rice, Wayne. *Hot Illustrations for Youth Talks* on CD-ROM Version 1.0. Grand Rapids, MI: Zondervan, 2001.

MEN AT WORK: LEADING IN MINISTRY

1. Jesus, the Ultimate Man, was a servant.

   ...so he got up from the meal, took off his outer clothing, and wrapped a towel around his waist. After that, he poured water into a basin and began to wash his disciples' feet, drying them with the towel that was wrapped around him.... When he had finished washing their feet, he put on his clothes and returned to his place. "Do you understand what I have done for you?" he asked them. "You call me 'Teacher' and 'Lord,' and rightly so, for that is what I am. Now that I, your Lord and Teacher, have washed your feet, you also should wash one another's feet. I have set you an example that you should do as I have done for you. Very truly I tell you, servants are not greater than their master, nor are messengers greater than the one who sent them. Now that you know these things, you will be blessed if you do them. (John 13:4-5, 12-17)

   (Jesus was the Ultimate Man and showed us what it means to be a man. It's not about how cool, smart, funny, or rich you are. It's about serving others. It's about helping people and serving people. That's what we were CREATED to do.)

2. You were created for ministry.

   "For we are God's handiwork, created in Christ Jesus to do good works, which God prepared in advance for us to do." (Ephesians 2:10)

   (You were created for ministry, for good works. God made you to play the game. You were meant to play on the field, not sit on the bench. Being a man means being part of the team. And everyone has something to do or give—just as the first followers of Jesus did when the church began.

Read Acts 6:1-4.

   In those days when the number of disciples was increasing, the Hellenistic Jews among them complained against the Hebraic Jews because their widows were being overlooked in the daily distribution of food. So the Twelve gathered all the disciples together and said, "It would not be right for us to neglect the ministry of the word of God in order to wait on tables. Brothers and sisters, choose seven men from among you who are known to be full of the Spirit and wisdom. We will turn this responsibility over to them and will give our attention to prayer and the ministry of the word."

The disciples have a problem. Widows are being overlooked. The disciples already have a ministry of telling people about Jesus. But who's going to take care of the widows? No problem. They just create a new ministry.

In the same way we have two kinds of ministries today: stuff already happening and stuff that needs to happen.)

3. Two different kinds of ministries:

A. Stuff already <u>happening</u>

(In the Acts passage, the disciples are already teaching people about Jesus. This is already happening and going great. Similarly, many ministries or opportunities to serve others are already taking place in churches all over.)

Some examples of ministries or areas of service your church might already have:

▷ Teaching

▷ Preaching

▷ Singing or choir

▷ Playing an instrument

▷ Reader

▷ Prayer leader

▷ Usher

▷ Communion helper

▷ Acolyte

▷ Child care helper

▷ Vacation Bible school teacher or assistant

▷ Sound

▷ Lighting

▷ Video

▷ Setup

▷ Teardown

▷ Greeter

▷ Hospital visitation

▷ In-home Communion server

▷ Other:

B. Stuff that <u>isn't yet</u> happening

(In the Acts passage it's great people are learning about Jesus, but the poor widows are getting hungry. Everyone wants to tell others about Jesus, which is fantastic! But these ladies still need food. No problem. They just create a new ministry to help the widows.

You can find so many ways to help other people and serve God. And while many ministries are already happening, much more needs to be done.)

Here's just a short list of some ways or areas to serve in that might not be happening at your church or in your community yet:

▷ Calling visitors

▷ Sending birthday cards

▷ Sending an e-mail newsletter

▷ Student ministry blog

▷ Prayer team

▷ Adopt a grandparent

▷ Lawn mowing ministry

▷ Volunteer janitor

▷ Umbrella ministry

▷ Care packages for college or sick students

▷ Snow team to shovel snow

▷ Homeless shelter volunteer

▷ Adopt a kid through Compassion International

▷ Homeless coffee hour

▷ Nursing home choir

▷ AIDS education

▷ Photographer or videographer

▷ Computer question and answer person

Moving into Ministry

Circle your answers.

Right now I'm a:

Benchwarmer

Rookie

Pro

Superstar

But I want to be a:

Rookie

Pro

Superstar

Circle your top three choices of ministry on the lists or write your ministry ideas here:

MEN AT WORK: LEADING IN MINISTRY

1. J_____, the _____ man, was a s_____.

   > ...so he got up from the meal, took off his outer clothing, and wrapped a towel around his waist. After that, he poured water into a basin and began to wash his disciples' feet, drying them with the towel that was wrapped around him.... When he had finished washing their feet, he put on his clothes and returned to his place. "Do you understand what I have done for you?" he asked them. "You call me 'Teacher' and 'Lord,' and rightly so, for that is what I am. Now that I, your Lord and Teacher, have washed your feet, you also should wash one another's feet. I have set you an example that you should do as I have done for you. Very truly I tell you, servants are not greater than their master, nor are messengers greater than the one who sent them. Now that you know these things, you will be blessed if you do them. (John 13:4-5, 12-17)

2. You were created for m_____.

   > For we are God's handiwork, created in Christ Jesus to do good works, which God prepared in advance for us to do. (Ephesians 2:10)

3. Two different kinds of ministries:

A. Stuff already _____

Some examples of ministries or areas of service your church might already have:

- Teaching
- Preaching
- Singing or choir
- Playing an instrument
- Reader
- Prayer leader
- Usher
- Communion helper
- Acolyte
- Child care helper
- Vacation Bible School teacher or assistant
- Sound
- Lighting
- Video
- Setup
- Teardown
- Greeter
- Hospital visitation
- In-home Communion server
- Other: _____

2. Stuff that _____ happening

   Here's just a short list of some ways or areas to serve in that might not be happening at your church or in your community yet:

   ▷ Calling visitors

   ▷ Sending birthday cards

   ▷ Sending an e-mail newsletter

   ▷ Student ministry blog

   ▷ Prayer team

   ▷ Adopt a grandparent

   ▷ Lawn mowing ministry

   ▷ Volunteer janitor

   ▷ Umbrella ministry

   ▷ Care packages for college or sick students

   ▷ Snow team to shovel snow

   ▷ Homeless shelter volunteer

   ▷ Adopt a kid through Compassion International

   ▷ Homeless coffee hour

   ▷ Nursing home choir

   ▷ AIDS education

   ▷ Photographer or videographer

   ▷ Computer question and answer person

Moving into Ministry

Circle your answers.

Right now I'm a:	But I want to be a:
Benchwarmer	Rookie
Rookie	Pro
Pro	Superstar
Superstar	

Circle your top three choices of ministry on the lists above or write your ministry idea here:

MOVING INTO MINISTRY

BENCHWARMER

Someone who isn't involved in ministry of any kind. He's not playing the game—just sitting on the bench and keeping it warm.

ROOKIE

Anyone can be a rookie. All it takes is getting off the bench and getting involved in a ministry already happening. A rookie is someone who isn't really ready to lead. But he does want to get involved in ministry. He needs someone to direct him and show him the ropes.

First check out what's going on in your church, school, or community already (greeting, ushering, reading Scripture, washing your youth pastor's car, helping at a soup kitchen, etc.) and pick a ministry to join.

Call whoever's in charge of the ministry and tell her you'd like to join the team and ask her when you can start. Then do it.

PRO

The difference between a rookie and a pro is, a rookie needs direction and a pro leads the way. A pro is a leader. You have two ways to be a pro:

1. Find a ministry already going on. Be part of it. Eventually, if it makes sense and works out, lead or help lead that ministry. Organize it. Get other rookies (whether students or adults) to join it.

2. Sometimes the ministry you want to do doesn't exist. A pro thinks of some way to make a difference or some need that's not being met and creates and leads a new ministry.

SUPERSTAR

The superstar level of ministry is when you can create a ministry (without a lot of help) based on one or all of the following:

▷ Something you love to do

▷ Something you're good at

▷ Some experience in your past, good or bad

See the superstar examples on the back of this sheet.

SUPERSTAR EXAMPLES

Zach Hunter

(remember him from your **Soul Work**?)

Zach did a report on slavery and was saddened by it (experience).

He wrote a paper about it (something he's good at).

He loves telling people about what they can do to end slavery.

Zach's all-star ministry: He created a ministry called LC2LC, Loose Change to Loosen Chains.

Albert Pujols

(first baseman for the 2006 World Champion St. Louis Cardinals)

Albert loves to help other people.

Albert is VERY good at baseball.

Albert's daughter has Down syndrome (experience).

Albert's all-star ministry: The Pujols Family Foundation gives money to several charities, including the Down Syndrome Association of Greater St. Louis.

Steve "Jake" Jacobs

(chief scientist for the Discovery Channel)

Jake loves to teach, making complex problems easier.

Jake is great at making TV shows.

Jake was humiliated and made fun of as a kid (experience).

Jake's all-star ministry: Jake was able to raise millions of dollars on television to fund research to find a cure for leprosy, a skin disease found in the poorest areas of the world.

Wild Truth Bible Lessons:
Dares from Jesus
Mark Oestreicher
$12.99
ISBN 0-310-24187-1

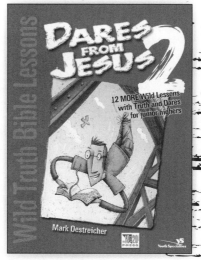

Wild Truth Bible Lessons:
Dares from Jesus 2
Mark Oestreicher
$12.99
ISBN 0-310-25050-1

Dares From Jesus 1 & 2 each provide twelve Bible lessons to help middle school students get their hands around some of these holy challenges such as forgiveness, telling the truth, taking responsibility, and more.

The student journal is a collection of 50 calls-to-action to get your kids moving toward God.

Wild Truth Journal:
Dares from Jesus
Mark Oestreicher
$9.99
ISBN 0-310-24189-8

YS youth specialties

Designed for middle schoolers, this engaging study will help students learn about temptation, the Holy Spirit's power to help, and what God desires from them. With questions that meet the developmental and spiritual needs of early adolescents, you'll find that your students engage in the Deeper studies and really grasp the lessons.

Choose
Steer Wide of Total Stupidity
Kevin Johnson
$7.99
ISBN 0-310-27493-1

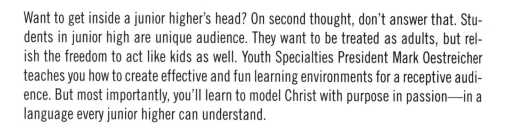